This Journal Belongs to

....

Josh Mosey

The 5-Minute BIBLE STUDY JOURNAL for Dads

BARBOUR
PUBLISHING™

YOU are the reason we do what we do here at Barbour Publishing. We promise that we will always use our God-given talents to produce content with you in mind—and that we will remain biblically faithful, no matter what.

Thank you for being the heart of our business.

Print ISBN 979-8-89151-283-2

Text previously published as *The 5-Minute Bible Study for Dads*, published by Barbour Publishing, Inc.

Published by Barbour Publishing, Inc., 1810 Barbour Drive, Uhrichsville, Ohio 44683, www.barbourbooks.com

Our mission is to inspire the world with the life-changing message of the Bible.

Printed in China.

INTRODUCTION

You're busy. Of course you're busy! You're a dad! And as a dad, you want to raise your kids well. God wants that for you too.

For our kids to recognize our Father in heaven, it helps to have an earthly father who acts like Him. To do that well is going to take commitment, effort, and wisdom. In short, it's going to take God's Word. This book is designed to help guys like you dig into the Bible and get what you need to be a great dad—even if you have only five minutes!

- Minutes 1–2: ***Read.*** Dig into the full scripture passage for each day's Bible study.
- Minute 3: ***Understand.*** Ponder a couple of prompts designed to help you apply the verses from the Bible to your own life. Consider these throughout your day as well.
- Minute 4: ***Apply.*** Read a brief devotional based on the day's scripture. Think about what you are learning and how to apply the scriptural truths to your own life, then journal your thoughts in the space below.
- Minute 5: ***Pray.*** A prayer starter will help you to begin a time of conversation with God. Remember to allow time for Him to speak into your life as well.

May *The 5-Minute Bible Study Journal for Dads* help you to establish the discipline of studying God's Word. Pour yourself a cup of coffee, grab your Bible, and make that first five minutes of your day count! You will find that even five minutes focused on scripture and prayer has the power to make a huge difference, not just for you but for your kids too. When you apply the scripture to your life, you'll be more like your Father in heaven. And when you get into the habit of studying the Bible, you'll want to spend even more time in God's Word!

EMBRACE THE ROUTINE

Read Daniel 6:1–22

KEY VERSE:

Now when Daniel learned that the decree had been published, he went home to his upstairs room where the windows opened toward Jerusalem. Three times a day he got down on his knees and prayed, giving thanks to his God, just as he had done before.

DANIEL 6:10 NIV

UNDERSTAND:

Think about the situation Daniel was in. He oversaw the collection of tributes from all over the kingdom. The temptation to use his office for personal gain must have been there. Why didn't Daniel succumb to temptation?

....

....

....

How does your routine include time for God?

....

....

....

Do others know about your relationship with God by the way you spend your time?

....

....

....

APPLY:

The story of Daniel in the lions' den is well known. The king appointed one hundred twenty satraps—or rulers—over the kingdom, with Daniel as their boss. Motivated by jealousy or to use the tributes they collected in unscrupulous ways, the satraps looked for ways to denounce Daniel, but the man was too faithful for accusations to stick!

In the end, the satraps used Daniel's faithfulness to God to send him to the lions' den. It was God's faithfulness in return that led Daniel out, safe and sound.

Faithfulness is a two-way street. Daniel showed his commitment to God through his daily routine and faultless lifestyle. A predictable routine not only helps us stay focused on God, but it can also provide comfort to our kids by knowing what to expect.

Build your routine. Commit to practices that honor God. Your routine may not keep you from the lions' den, but your faithfulness will keep you safe.

....

....

....

....

....

....

....

....

PRAY:

Heavenly Father, You shut the mouths of the lions because Daniel refused to be silenced. May the ways I spend my time be predictable to my kids and honoring to You. Keep me from being tempted to bend my routine when it gets uncomfortable. Amen.

SEEK WISDOM AND UNDERSTANDING

Read Proverbs 2

KEY VERSE:

For the LORD giveth wisdom: out of his mouth cometh knowledge and understanding.

PROVERBS 2:6 KJV

UNDERSTAND:

According to Proverbs 2:1–5, what are the prerequisites to understanding the fear of the Lord and finding the knowledge of God?

According to Proverbs 2:20–22, what are the benefits of walking with wisdom and understanding?

What are some instances in which you wish you had acted with more wisdom? How would understanding the situation better have changed things?

APPLY:

The book of Proverbs is full of wise sayings, but wisdom is more than pithy quotes. Wisdom is the right application of knowledge with a full understanding of how it is applied. Dads like you need wisdom ALL THE TIME. But how do you get it?

Today's key verse identifies the source of all wisdom—the Lord—but accessing wisdom is more than knowing that God is wise. Proverbs 2:4 (ESV) says that wisdom is found when "you seek it like silver and search for it as for hidden treasures." It is a partnership of intense effort—mining it from God's Word, His people, and through prayer—and a recognition that it is a gift from God.

So meditate on the wisdom God has shared with you thus far. Pray for wisdom when you face troublesome parenting situations with your kids. Then listen to His Spirit for guidance.

PRAY:

Lord, You are the giver of wisdom. Help me realize my need for Your knowledge and perspective. Help me seek Your wisdom with intentional effort. Give me what I need to help my kids grow in wisdom too. Amen.

REDEFINE SUCCESS

Read Philippians 3

KEY VERSE:

Indeed, I count everything as loss because of the surpassing worth of knowing Christ Jesus my Lord. For his sake I have suffered the loss of all things and count them as rubbish, in order that I may gain Christ.

PHILIPPIANS 3:8 ESV

UNDERSTAND:

Consider Paul's qualifications from Philippians 3:4–7. How does the modern world define success?

....

....

....

The praise of the world can be a powerful motivator. Why shouldn't you base your definition of success on worldly praise?

....

....

....

....

What does success look like for you as a dad who follows Christ?

....

....

....

....

APPLY:

If anyone could brag about living a successful life, Paul could. In Philippians 3, Paul lists the reasons why, according to appearances, he was the pinnacle of religious success. But he goes on to say that these things that set him apart for earthly praise are rubbish—literally dung or garbage—compared to what true success is: knowing Christ.

If your goal is to look like you've got it all together, you've got the wrong goal. If your definition of success is based on what other people (including your kids) think about you, you will never be truly successful.

Your goal is to press on toward God's call. Success is letting go of the past and embracing the future. To be a successful dad, don't dwell on the mistakes you've made. Hold firmly to the love of Christ, and show your kids what can happen when a dad loves others self-sacrificially.

PRAY:

Heavenly Father, may I be motivated by my love for You and sustained by Your love for me. Help me rethink what success means and show my children that knowing You is more important than the praise of this world. Amen.

GET SPIRITUALLY DRESSED

Read Colossians 3:1–15

KEY VERSE:

Therefore, as God's chosen people, holy and dearly loved, clothe yourselves with compassion, kindness, humility, gentleness and patience.

Colossians 3:12 NIV

UNDERSTAND:

You're supposed to be dead to sin and alive in Christ. How can you practically put to death the practices mentioned in verses 5–9?

....

....

....

How might you update the list of opposing groups of people from verse 11?

....

....

....

Name at least one person who comes to mind when you read the list of attributes in today's key verse. If possible, write that person a message to let them know you appreciate their example.

....

....

....

....

APPLY:

Every dad puts on pants one leg at a time—unless he wears a kilt or has a fancy way of getting dressed. The point is that getting dressed is an everyday occurrence you probably don't have to put too much effort into. Even less if you wear a uniform, because the outfit is already picked out for you.

The list of attributes from today's verse is much like a uniform. It's the identifiable way the world can see Christ living inside you. That doesn't mean that Christians never struggle with compassion, kindness, humility, gentleness, or patience. Kids can test the patience of every father! But when you put on the uniform of these Christian attributes, belting it all on with Christ's love, it's a natural—but intentional—act.

Spend some time in prayer ironing out your spiritual outfit. Be extra patient with your kids and let them see how a Christian dad is dressed.

PRAY:

Lord God, show me the ways I'm not dressed well today. Give me the patience and kindness I need to show my children Your love. Keep me from bringing to life the sins You died to save me from. Amen.

READ YOUR BIBLE HABITUALLY

Read Joshua 1

KEY VERSE:

"This Book of the Law shall not depart from your mouth, but you shall meditate on it day and night, so that you may be careful to do according to all that is written in it. For then you will make your way prosperous, and then you will have good success."

JOSHUA 1:8 ESV

UNDERSTAND:

The phrase "Be strong and courageous" is mentioned multiple times in God's instructions to Joshua as he fills Moses' leadership role. Although God assures Joshua He will be with him (verse 5), the task Joshua faced was daunting. In which areas of your life do you need to "be strong and courageous"?

....

....

....

Where does your mind wander when left to its own devices?

....

....

....

Write down one verse from today's passage to meditate on today.

....

....

....

APPLY:

As Joshua prepared to lead the Israelites out of the wilderness and into the Promised Land, God gave him encouragement and a call to action. Joshua 1:9 (ESV) says, "Have I not commanded you? Be strong and courageous. Do not be frightened, and do not be dismayed, for the LORD your God is with you wherever you go."

To be equipped for the battles ahead, God told Joshua to meditate on the Law all the time and to walk forward in faith. Today, we have more of God's Word than Joshua had, plus we have the Holy Spirit dwelling inside us, but the orders are still the same: Meditate on God's truth and walk forward in faith.

No matter the battles you are facing today—mental or emotional struggles, problems at work, or strained relationships with your kids—God is with you. Only be strong and courageous. Don't dwell on the troubles; dwell on God's Word.

PRAY:

Lord, I trust that You are with me. May I walk with courage and strength as I focus on You. Bind my thoughts to Your Word and my actions to Your will. Help me trust You, even while I face the battles in my life, because You are bigger than the problems I face. Amen.

SPEND TIME ON THINGS THAT MATTER

Read Ephesians 5:1–21

KEY VERSES:

Be very careful, then, how you live—
not as unwise but as wise, making the most of
every opportunity, because the days are evil.
Ephesians 5:15–16 NIV

UNDERSTAND:

Today's passage talks about "sons of disobedience" and "children of light." How do the things on which you spend time show which family you belong to?

....

....

....

What are some ways you can make the most of your time?

....

....

....

How can you spend quality time with your kids in ways that honor God?

....

....

....

....

APPLY:

When Paul refers to the days being evil in today's key verse, he was writing about the times in which he lived. Unfortunately, the passage of time hasn't made the days any less evil. We still live in a world sodden with sin—sexual immorality, impurity, covetousness, crude joking, drunken debauchery—it's all still here.

So Paul tells us that Christians need to look at the ways we spend our time, at the things we make important to us. It isn't enough to claim Christ's sacrifice only to return to a life of selfish desires. We are called to be children of light who reflect God's love to the world around us.

As a dad, you show your children what is important to you every day by how you spend your time. Think about what they'll see you spending time on today, and give thanks to God for including you among His children.

PRAY:

Lord, may my kids see how important You are by the way I spend my time. Keep me from selfish pursuits that aren't honoring to You. May I reflect Your light into the world of darkness. Amen.

SHOW RESPECT TO ALL PEOPLE

Read Romans 12

KEY VERSE:

Be devoted to one another in love.
Honor one another above yourselves.
Romans 12:10 NIV

UNDERSTAND:

The first verse of today's passage calls Christians to present their bodies as living sacrifices to God as spiritual worship. What does it mean to you to be a living sacrifice?

....

....

....

....

Romans 12:9–21 presents a variety of instructions for Christian living. In which areas do you struggle the most?

....

....

....

....

How can you pray to invite God to work in these areas?

....

....

....

....

APPLY:

In stories, narrative is driven by conflict. Man is pitted against man, nature, self, or society. The story of the Bible is driven by man's conflict with God, the results of which have led to every other form of conflict imaginable. God did not pick the fight—man did—but because of God's love, He has made it possible for peace to rule in place of conflict.

When we allow the Spirit to transform us, we begin to see others the way God sees us. As such, we are called to show respect to everyone, both inside the church (see Romans 12:3–8) and with the public at large (see Romans 12:9–21).

The church is not called to treat unbelievers with disrespect but to show God's love to all. We are to try to live at peace with everyone because God's peace is to live within us. Today, let your kids see God's peace in you as you show respect to man, nature, self, and society.

PRAY:

Lord, let my love be genuine because it comes from You. Let it not be tainted by selfishness. Help me have opportunities to show honor to everyone around me. Make Your peace tangible to me as I seek to bring peace wherever conflict is found. Amen.

CHOOSE EMPATHY OVER SYMPATHY

Read John 11:17–44

KEY VERSE:

When Jesus saw her weeping, and the Jews who had come with her also weeping, he was deeply moved in his spirit and greatly troubled.

JOHN 11:33 ESV

UNDERSTAND:

The sisters of Lazarus—Martha and Mary—asked Jesus the same question. How did Jesus answer them differently?

....

....

....

Why did Jesus allow Lazarus to die and his loved ones to mourn if He could have prevented it? See John 11:40 for a clue.

....

....

....

When has God allowed you to experience pain only to show you His glory afterward?

....

....

....

....

APPLY:

Sympathy is when you share the feelings of another person. When someone is sad, you are sad for them. Empathy is when you understand someone intimately because you've experienced the same thing.

Today's passage includes the deity of Jesus—He called someone back to life days after the dead body had begun to rot—as well as His humanity—He wept human tears for the reality of death in this fallen world. Jesus didn't simply sympathize with Martha and Mary's grief; He felt it deeply because it was His own.

Being a good dad means going further than being sad when your kids are sad. It means setting aside your interests and remembering what it was like to be a kid. Empathize with your kids. Show them you understand in the same way that Jesus understands us.

PRAY:

Lord Jesus, You fully understand what it is to be human while being fully God and able to solve my human problems. Help me empathize with my kids as You have empathized with me. I pray that You would receive glory, even from my pain. Amen.

DISCIPLINE WELL

Read Hebrews 12:1–17

KEY VERSE:

Endure hardship as discipline; God is treating you as his children. For what children are not disciplined by their father?

HEBREWS 12:7 NIV

UNDERSTAND:

Hebrews 12 opens by imagining the heroes of the Old Testament gathered in a stadium to watch modern saints run the race of Christian living. This thought should both cheer us and help us understand the seriousness of our race. Your kids are watching you too. How is your race going?

What sins and hindrances should you throw off in order to run better?

How is endurance related to discipline?

APPLY:

Discipline is a word with many meanings. A parent might discipline a misbehaving child. Training for a marathon requires discipline. It can also refer to a course of study, as in "the discipline of mathematics." The shared root of all these meanings relates to the word *disciple*, or "one who is taught."

Learning experiences come in all forms. And while discipline and pain are often related, it should never be the goal to inflict pain when disciplining our kids. The goal is always to teach a better way with love, sparing as much pain from them as possible. Yes, God allows us to experience pain as we receive the natural consequences of our actions, but Jesus died to save us from the worst consequence: separation from God.

As you seek to correct the behavior of your kids, remember to love them like God loves you. The goal is to restore the relationship. Discipline, always, with love.

....

....

....

....

....

....

....

....

....

PRAY:

Lord, help me to learn what I need to when I experience painful correction. Help me to discipline my kids with love and grace. Give me wisdom to know how to teach them well. Amen.

LOVE YOUR WIFE

Read Ephesians 5:22–33

KEY VERSE:

In the same way husbands should love their wives as their own bodies. He who loves his wife loves himself.

Ephesians 5:28 ESV

UNDERSTAND:

Marriage reflects Christ's relationship with the church. In what ways do you identify with the wife's call in verses 22–24 to submit to Christ's leadership?

....

....

....

Name three recent instances when you've loved your wife self-sacrificially. If you are not married, how have you loved someone else self-sacrificially?

....

....

....

....

Why is it in a husband's interest to love his wife as he loves his own body?

....

....

....

....

APPLY:

Marriage is the holy union of two individuals, a covenant between spouses in which each commits to love the other self-sacrificially. It's the oldest human relationship on the planet—starting with Adam and Eve—and the basis for society the world over. But marriage isn't really about two people in love; it is designed to be a reflection of God's relationship with humanity.

One of the best things you can do for your kids is to have a healthy, God-honoring relationship with your wife. If your marriage is truly a reflection of God's relationship with humanity, your kids will see marriage as an honorable and desirable thing. If your marriage reflects man's fallen, selfish nature, not only will they see marriage through the wrong lens, but they'll also lack the comfort that strong marriages provide.

Whether you are blissfully wed, blissfully unwed, or un-blissfully either, seek to live out your human relationships as a reflection of God's loving, self-sacrificial relationship with you.

PRAY:

Lord, You are committed to me. Help me be committed to You. You love me. Help me reflect that love in all of my relationships. Amen.

PRAY CONFIDENTLY ACCORDING TO GOD'S WILL

Read Mark 11:12–25

KEY VERSE:

"Therefore I tell you, whatever you ask in prayer, believe that you have received it, and it will be yours."
MARK 11:24 ESV

UNDERSTAND:

In the Old Testament (see Jeremiah 8:13; Hosea 9:10), the fig tree symbolized God's relationship with Israel. How does Jesus' interaction with the fig tree in today's passage relate to His cleansing of the temple in Jerusalem?

The Jews expected the Messiah to bring Israel out of servitude to the Gentiles and restore the temple to exclusively Jewish use. How did Jesus defy these expectations?

APPLY:

Fig trees are common throughout lands of the Bible. In Judea, fig trees start growing fruit around the same time as their foliage, so if a fig tree has large leaves, it would be reasonable to assume it has a lot of fruit as well. The episode with the fig tree in today's passage is an indictment of Israel's temple for appearing to be healthy while bearing no real fruit. As such, both the fig tree and temple were destined for destruction.

The point of a fig tree is to grow figs, to feed those who need nourishment. How does this relate to prayer? God wants us to live fruit-filled lives to nourish the world around us. He'll gladly equip us to do His will when we pray confidently for guidance and the means to do so.

Is your prayer life bearing fruit, or is it a tree full of leaves and disappointment?

PRAY:

Lord, You've promised in Your Word to supply every need according to Your riches, not so I can become rich but so I can do Your will on earth. Help me see the needs around me. Make me fruitful so I can nourish others. Amen.

LOVE AND BE FAITHFUL

Read Proverbs 3

KEY VERSES:

Let love and faithfulness never leave you; bind them around your neck, write them on the tablet of your heart. Then you will win favor and a good name in the sight of God and man.

Proverbs 3:3–4 NIV

UNDERSTAND:

Proverbs 3 is full, not only of advice but of reasons to listen to the advice. What are some of the listed benefits of listening to the proverb writer's wisdom?

....

....

....

How do you write something "on the tablet of your heart"?

....

....

....

....

How can you "honor the Lord with your wealth" (Proverbs 3:9 NIV)?

....

....

....

....

APPLY:

In Exodus 34:6 (NIV), after God had given Moses the Ten Commandments, He told Moses His name: "And he passed in front of Moses, proclaiming, 'The LORD, the LORD, the compassionate and gracious God, slow to anger, abounding in love and faithfulness.'"

Love and faithfulness are part of God's character, His identity. For us to show the world whom we belong to, we are called to show these character traits. But doing so does not happen without intention. We are to actively safeguard love and faithfulness, to bind them around our neck and write them on the tablet of our heart.

Without action, the love we feel for God will fade to indifference, and the faithfulness by which we live will turn into selfishness. Don't let yourself drift from who God has called you to be. Stay in love with God. Be faithful to Him. When you do, you'll win favor and a good name in the sight of God and man.

PRAY:

Father God, You are love itself. You are wholly faithful to me. Don't let me drift toward selfish indifference. May I be active in my love and faithfulness to You. Amen.

SHOW, DON'T TELL

Read James 2:14–36

KEY VERSE:

What good is it, my brothers, if someone says he has faith but does not have works? Can that faith save him?

James 2:14 ESV

UNDERSTAND:

Today's passage lists two Old Testament examples of people whose faith resulted in works. What are some other examples of biblical heroes who acted out of faith?

....

....

....

Can you think of any examples of people who had genuine faith without acting on it?

....

....

....

....

If someone were to look at the actions of your life, would they identify your faith as genuine?

....

....

....

....

APPLY:

It is only by faith that a person is saved. There's nothing inside us, no action we can take, no amount of "good living" we can do to merit God's grace. It is only by God's love and Jesus' sacrifice that we're able to come to faith at all. But is faith on its own enough?

James wrote today's passage to help believers think through this question. The conclusion he comes to—the one we all should come to—is that genuine faith will necessarily result in action. If we have accepted God's gift of salvation through faith, we *can't help* but show our faith by the things we do.

As a dad, you love your kids, and that love leads you toward actions that highlight that love. You pay attention when they talk, protect them from harm, and give them good gifts. Telling them you love them without acting it out is useless. It's the same way with God.

PRAY:

Lord, I know that my works will never merit Your love for me. Still, may the world know I am Yours by my works. Help me love my kids with my words and my actions, just like I am called to love You. Amen.

SET BOUNDARIES FOR YOUR CHILDREN

Read Ephesians 6

KEY VERSE:

Fathers, do not provoke your children to anger, but bring them up in the discipline and instruction of the Lord.

EPHESIANS 6:4 ESV

UNDERSTAND:

Paul's message to the Ephesians that children should obey their parents wasn't new. Why might today's verse have struck them as revolutionary?

....

....

....

In Paul's message to bondservants and masters, each is called to serve the other since Christ is the master of both. How might you better serve those above and below you?

....

....

....

How can putting on the full armor of God (verses 11–17) make serving others easier?

....

....

....

APPLY:

Believe it or not, children thrive in predictable, rule-following settings. Research has shown that there is comfort in boundaries and restrictions. Kids who have too much freedom and too little guidance are more anxious than kids who know what to expect and when to expect it. Think of rules and boundaries like seat belts, designed not to restrict someone without reason but to keep them safe from harm.

So go ahead and give your kids some rules and boundaries! Consider things like curfews, screen time limits, and strict internet controls. Then, when you put a boundary in place, enforce it. Kids will naturally test the boundaries to see if they are there for a reason, just like they might lean against a seat belt to see if it will stop them.

But rules are only part of the equation. Kids require instruction as well. Teach them the benefits of living according to God's Word. Even better, show them by how you live.

PRAY:

Lord, give me wisdom when setting up rules for my family to obey. Help me instill in them the understanding that boundaries exist to help us thrive, not to deprive us of freedom. Let them see a good example in me. Amen.

SET BOUNDARIES FOR YOURSELF

Read Galatians 5

KEY VERSES:

This I say then, Walk in the Spirit, and ye shall not fulfil the lust of the flesh. For the flesh lusteth against the Spirit, and the Spirit against the flesh: and these are contrary the one to the other: so that ye cannot do the things that ye would.

GALATIANS 5:16–17 KJV

UNDERSTAND:

After reading today's passage, how would you define "freedom"?

How does yesterday's passage (Ephesians 6:10–18) equip believers to resist the works of the flesh listed in today's passage (Galatians 5:19–21)?

How can you better prepare the soil of your heart to grow the fruit of the Spirit? How can you daily crucify the desires of the flesh?

APPLY:

Yesterday, we covered why boundaries and rules can help kids thrive. The same is true for us. In today's passage, we learn that freedom is not a lack of rules but submission to the right rules.

Galatians 5:1 (ESV) says, "For freedom Christ has set us free; stand firm therefore, and do not submit again to a yoke of slavery." The truth is that we will always be subservient to something. When we serve our fallen desires, we reap harvests of troubles. But when we serve the Lord, we grow the fruit of the Spirit.

What boundaries have you set up to safeguard yourself from self-inflicted harm? Just as you came up with rules for your kids regarding screen time and internet safety, come up with rules for yourself. You know the areas in which you are weak. Invite God into those areas and listen to the Spirit's prompting regarding boundaries that will help you cultivate the right fruit.

....

....

....

....

....

....

....

....

....

....

PRAY:

Lord, grow the right fruit in my life.
Keep me from cultivating my selfish desires.
Bring someone into my life who can keep me
accountable for the boundaries I set. Amen.

MEMORIZE SCRIPTURE

Read Psalm 119:1–48

KEY VERSE:

Thy word have I hid in mine heart,
that I might not sin against thee.
Psalm 119:11 KJV

UNDERSTAND:

Psalm 119 is a carefully crafted piece of poetry, the first letter of each stanza beginning with each letter in the Hebrew alphabet in order. It is also the longest psalm and the longest chapter in the Bible. Why do you think it was written?

The psalmist returns throughout to the theme of God's truth. Which truth stands out to you as you read?

Which Bible verses have you already hidden in your heart?

APPLY:

Does the Bible keep us from sin, or does sin keep us from the Bible? It's an old question that recognizes the antithetical nature of God's Word and sin. Throughout the length of this book, you are reading and studying verses meant to lead you into a closer relationship with God and a deeper understanding of yourself as His follower and representative. After all, there is no distinction between God's Word and Himself.

John 1:1 (KJV) says, "In the beginning was the Word, and the Word was with God, and the Word was God."

By committing God's Word to our memory, we're doing for our minds what the Spirit does for our souls—filling and focusing our identities with God's transforming power. When we are full of scripture, we are better prepared to fight the lies of sin with God's truths.

Today, make a list of verses that you feel would better prepare you for the fight, and start committing them to memory.

PRAY:

Father God, You've given me salvation through Your Son, help and comfort through Your Spirit, and truth itself in Your Word. Help me commit Your truth to memory so I am protected from sin's temptations. Amen.

SET AN EXAMPLE

Read 1 Peter 2

KEY VERSE:

To this you were called, because Christ suffered for you, leaving you an example, that you should follow in his steps.
1 PETER 2:21 NIV

UNDERSTAND:

Peter compares an infant's longing for milk to the believer's longing for God's Word. How can this "spiritual milk" help you grow in the Lord?

....

....

....

Jesus is the foundation on which Christianity is built, but Christianity doesn't call us to separate ourselves from nonbelievers. What does Peter recommend in verses 13–17?

....

....

....

....

How does suffering unjustly reveal God's gospel life in you?

....

....

....

....

APPLY:

In today's passage, Peter says that Christ left us an example of how to suffer well when we are accused unjustly of sins. "When they hurled their insults at him, he did not retaliate; when he suffered, he made no threats. Instead, he entrusted himself to him who judges justly" (1 Peter 2:23 NIV).

Jesus was our example in many ways. He spoke truth to power, had compassion on those whom society did not value, and loved everyone self-sacrificially and unconditionally.

As a father, your children will grow up watching the example you set. You will hear your words come out of their mouths and watch them act like you do. You can set no better example for them than to mimic the example set by Christ.

Pay attention today to your words, both the ones you say when things are going well and the ones that slip out when you suffer. Listen to your kids and see if you are setting the example you'd like them to follow.

PRAY:

Jesus, thank You for being the example for me. Help me be a good example for my children. Help me suffer well and refrain from retaliation or unclean words. May I see in my kids the areas of my life that give You the most pleasure. Amen.

TREAT PEOPLE EQUITABLY

Read James 2:1–13

KEY VERSE:

My brothers and sisters, believers in our glorious Lord Jesus Christ must not show favoritism.

JAMES 2:1 NIV

UNDERSTAND:

James writes about a situation in which a rich man is given a prominent place at a house church, while a poor man was treated with contempt. What are some modern parallels of this situation?

....

....

....

James 2:8 mentions the "royal law" about loving your neighbor as yourself. How does James' message relate to Jesus' parable of the good Samaritan (Luke 10:25–37)?

....

....

....

How have you been guilty of showing partiality toward a certain race or social class?

....

....

....

....

APPLY:

Today's passage warns believers not to show favoritism—giving preferential treatment to someone based on external appearances like race, wealth, or clothing. This should be obvious to Christians based on the example and teachings of Jesus.

Whom did Jesus call to be His disciples? Fishermen, tax collectors, and zealots. Men who wouldn't have been chosen by any other rabbi.

Whom did Jesus spend the most time with? The poor, the infirm. People who lived on the bottom rung of society's ladder.

Whom did Jesus trade verbal barbs with? The religious elite. People who flaunted their power and wealth.

Never justify treating the privileged in society with greater deference than those with no external privileges. It isn't the rich and powerful who need the extra love.

Today, think through how you talk about people in power and those without. What opinions are your children hearing? Would Jesus approve of how equitably you treat people?

PRAY:

Lord, everyone is equal at the foot of the cross. Help me treat those who need help and love with respect. Help me keep those with power accountable for the way they wield it. May my children see the way I treat my neighbors and think of Your example. Amen.

TEACH YOUR KIDS WHAT YOU KNOW

Read Deuteronomy 11:1–25

KEY VERSES:

Love the Lord your God and keep his requirements, his decrees, his laws and his commands always. . . . Teach them to your children, talking about them when you sit at home and when you walk along the road, when you lie down and when you get up.

Deuteronomy 11:1, 19 NIV

UNDERSTAND:

In today's reading, Moses addresses those Israelites who witnessed firsthand the events of the Exodus and the wilderness, reminding them that they serve a powerful God who is worthy of obedience. How has God shown Himself to be powerful to you?

....

....

How can you teach your children about God's power and love?

....

....

....

Which commandment listed in today's reading is the most important to teach your kids?

....

....

....

APPLY:

Children are sponges. They are wired to learn as much as they can all the time. Babies quickly learn to associate sounds with actions and expectations. Toddlers come up with theories about how the world works based on what they observe.

Kids are knowledge magnets, and we live in the age of information. Television, the internet, books on almost any subject—kids learn in a variety of ways, but most of all, they learn by watching us.

If you spend more time watching the game on TV than discussing what God is doing in your life, your kids will prioritize the game. If you spend more time staring at social media than interacting with your kids face-to-face, they'll learn to prioritize screen time. If you've been teaching your kids the wrong things, it's not too late to change course. Love the Lord your God. Show them what that love can do. Teach them what is really important.

....

....

....

....

....

....

....

....

....

PRAY:

Lord, reprioritize my life so that You are the most important thing in it. Help me talk about You to my kids when I sit at home and when I walk along the road, when I lie down and when I get up. May my kids see loving You as their priority too. Amen.

BE VULNERABLE

Read 2 Corinthians 12

KEY VERSE:

But he said to me, "My grace is sufficient for you, for my power is made perfect in weakness." Therefore I will boast all the more gladly about my weaknesses, so that Christ's power may rest on me.
2 Corinthians 12:9 NIV

UNDERSTAND:

In 2 Corinthians 11, Paul says that false apostles have led the church at Corinth toward a different gospel. These false apostles, to whom Paul refers in today's passage, boasted in their speaking credentials and Jewish pedigree. How does that differ from Paul's boasting?

....

....

....

How does admitting weakness allow Christ's power to rest on you?

....

....

....

With whom might you share your weaknesses to get prayer and support?

....

....

....

....

APPLY:

In Paul's second letter to Corinth, he reprimanded the church for listening to false apostles. These false teachers made themselves a financial burden to the church and preached about a fake Jesus. These teachers may have seemed like the real deal based on "you get what you pay for" logic, but their pay-to-play tactics should have been a warning to the Corinthian believers.

True teaching starts with vulnerability. Paul's credentials to teach about Christianity's thriving life wasn't in how much he charged for the message but in how great Christ was in his weakness.

Popular culture hasn't changed much in the last two thousand years. People still give more weight to highly paid speakers who seem to have it all together. But no one has it all together!

Your kids don't need to think you are perfect to know you are worthy of being listened to. Be vulnerable with them. Let Christ's strength shine through your weakness. That's who you really want them to follow anyway, right?

....

....

....

....

....

....

....

PRAY:

Lord, keep me from following the wrong gospel or giving more weight to false teachers, because their message comes with a price tag. Teach me to share my vulnerability with other believers. Let my kids see where true strength comes from. Amen.

USE YOUR WORDS TO BUILD UP, NOT TEAR DOWN

Read Ephesians 4

KEY VERSE:

Let no corrupting talk come out of your mouths, but only such as is good for building up, as fits the occasion, that it may give grace to those who hear.

EPHESIANS 4:29 ESV

UNDERSTAND:

In today's passage, Paul discusses some differences between mature and immature believers. How does maturity in Christ lead to unity within the Christian body?

According to verses 17–32, how is the mature Christian called to live? Which practices on this list stand out as areas in which to grow? Write them on a note card for further meditation and prayer today.

APPLY:

It's amazing how certain words and phrases sound different when they come from our children's mouths. Things you never heard as questionable before suddenly cut through conversations like a foghorn. But it isn't just swear words and off-color phrases that count as "corrupting talk" from today's key verse.

For mature Christians, corrupting talk is anything that detracts from the message of Christ. It's the white lies, false praise, and jokes you wouldn't tell your mom. It's name-calling, destructive self-talk, and gossip. Never forget: Words have power.

You are called to be like Christ, to live self-sacrificial lives of holiness. Reinforce your lifestyle with your words. Speak to others, to your kids, and to yourself in ways that build up instead of tear down. Praise what is praiseworthy. Lovingly correct what isn't.

Your kids need to hear heaven's speech from your lips, lest their ears go itching for the world's version of love.

PRAY:

Lord, may my words be wholesome and my lifestyle be honoring to You. Keep corruption from my speech so my kids will hear Your truths instead. Help me build them up to be followers of You. Amen.

HAVE FUN

Read Zechariah 8:1–17

KEY VERSE:

And the streets of the city shall be full of boys and girls playing in the streets thereof.

ZECHARIAH 8:5 KJV

UNDERSTAND:

The book of Zechariah is akin to Revelation as a book of futuristic prophecy. In the years after Israel's return from exile, the temple was only partially rebuilt, the taxes from Persia were high, and the people were discouraged. How might the people have heard Zechariah's vision of Jerusalem's future peace and prosperity from today's passage?

How are you communicating the peace and prosperity offered by life in Jesus to your kids?

APPLY:

The history of God's interaction with Israel in the Old Testament was somewhat cyclical. God affirmed His love for Israel. Israel went astray. God allowed Israel to be conquered. Israel turned back to God. And repeat.

Zechariah's visions, recorded in today's passage, are reaffirmation of God's love to Israel's people. They are promises that better days are coming to those who wait upon the Lord. Like all apocalyptic literature, Zechariah must be read with care, but here's what happened in the years after his visions were recorded:

Jesus Christ came to earth. He died and rose again, making it possible for the Holy Spirit to dwell within believers. People—not just Israel but all people—are offered the peace and eternal prosperity that come with life in Christ.

Since we have received these blessings already, it isn't too early for us to live accordingly. So go play with your kids. Show them that God keeps His promises and offers us life to the fullest.

....

....

....

....

....

....

....

....

PRAY:

Lord God, thank You for making a way for me to be at peace with You. Thank You for sending the Holy Spirit to live inside me. Help me enjoy the benefits of Your love while playing with my kids. Amen.

BOOST YOUR EQ

Read Ecclesiastes 3

KEY VERSE:

A time to weep, and a time to laugh;
a time to mourn, and a time to dance.
ECCLESIASTES 3:4 KJV

UNDERSTAND:

The poem in Ecclesiastes 3:1–8 is well-known, encompassing man's experiences through opposing ideas and situations. Throughout the book, the author seeks meaning and purpose in man's efforts but concludes that only what God does will last (verse 14). How does this truth affect your efforts and experiences?

How can you participate in something that will last beyond the span of your years?

APPLY:

It's strange how God invades the world. It shouldn't be. God is the Creator and sustainer, the reason and method by which everything exists. But when His Word reaches number one on the *Billboard* Hot 100 chart—as it did on December 4, 1965, with the Byrds' rendition of Ecclesiastes 3:1–8—it feels strange.

Even in folk-rock form, this passage resonates. It says that humanity is complex, that we feel different things at different times. But men sometimes struggle with this. We're fine with the time to laugh but don't take time to weep. We think the time to embrace is reserved for women, that we have to be stoic all the time.

If you want kids who deal with emotions in healthy ways, you need to embrace the whole of what it means to be human. Raise your emotional intelligence—your EQ—by acknowledging your feelings as you feel them but not allowing them to control your actions.

PRAY:

Father God, turn me from a simplistic view of emotions. Help me recognize the need for each feeling I encounter. Help me model emotional intelligence to my kids so they are not mastered by their feelings but by their need for You. Amen.

BE UNITED BY FAITH

Read Galatians 3

KEY VERSE:

There is neither Jew nor Greek, there is neither slave nor free, there is no male and female, for you are all one in Christ Jesus.

GALATIANS 3:28 ESV

UNDERSTAND:

In first century Galatia, identities like national origin, economic status, and gender dictated how people interacted with each other. How is that similar or different to life today?

How would the original audience have received Paul's message from today's key verse?

The law was given to reveal man's need for Jesus' gift of salvation. Are you living as a grateful recipient of that gift or laboring to fulfill the law on your own?

APPLY:

Status has always been important—it's why people compete on shows like *American Idol*—but status has been important for way longer than million-dollar record contracts have been around. The appeal to be given godlike status was part of the devil's appeal in the Garden of Eden. We've always wanted to be part of the "in crowd."

What if the "in crowd" was an illusion? Paul's letter to the church in Galatia was written to correct them for listening to false teachers who claimed that to be good Christians, they needed to be following the Jewish law. In other words, to be part of God's "in crowd," they needed to work harder. But that's not how grace works!

God's "in crowd" isn't made up of a specific race or gender or tax bracket. Because of Jesus' sacrifice, we're all on the same level in the eyes of grace. We should seek to treat everyone as worthy of God's love.

....

....

....

....

....

....

....

....

....

PRAY:

God, give me love for everyone. Help me strive not for worldly status but to bring all people to You. May I show my kids that grace is available to everyone, regardless of national origin, gender, or wealth. Amen.

LISTEN WELL

Read James 1

KEY VERSE:

My dear brothers and sisters, take note of this: Everyone should be quick to listen, slow to speak and slow to become angry.

James 1:19 NIV

UNDERSTAND:

According to James 1, what are the benefits of being steadfast under trials and hardships?

....

....

....

What practical advice does James give regarding God's Word and its application?

....

....

....

....

How can you grow your steadfast commitment to God, even when things are not going your way?

....

....

....

....

APPLY:

The book of James was written by James the Just, brother of Jesus. Can you imagine what it must have been like to be Jesus' little brother? He wouldn't have given you a hard time, but He set the bar impossibly high for good behavior.

Having grown up with Jesus, James would have had opportunities to hear Him speak well before He began his formal ministry. But hearing and listening are different. Listening involves paying attention, echoing back what you hear to make sure you understand, then acting in response to that knowledge. This is the kind of listening James writes about in today's verse.

James must have listened to Jesus. He was among the first people Jesus saw after the resurrection, and he went on to lead Jerusalem's church. How can you listen to God's Word like James? How can you better listen to your kids?

....

....

....

....

....

....

....

....

....

PRAY:

Lord, as an adopted child of God, I am Your brother like James was. Help me listen well when You speak to me through Your Word. Help me apply those listening skills to the people around me so they feel the value You've placed within them. Amen.

VALUE EVERY MOMENT

Read Psalm 39

KEY VERSE:

Lord, make me to know mine end, and the measure of my days, what it is: that I may know how frail I am.

Psalm 39:4 KJV

UNDERSTAND:

Today's passage, written by David, recognizes how the consequences of sin can make our short lives unbearable. Examine your heart and confess your sins to God. Use Psalm 39:7–13 as a prayer guide.

....

....

....

....

David talks about the futility of heaping up wealth (verse 6) in life. How might you better use your wealth for God's kingdom?

....

....

....

....

What things do you want your kids to know before it is too late?

....

....

....

....

APPLY:

In today's psalm, David is afflicted by sin. He doesn't want to cry out against God in the presence of the wicked, but his heart burns within him. When he can keep silent no longer, he begs God to deliver him.

David recognized that life is too short to be miserable because of sin. No matter how old you are, time is ticking down on your earthly clock. Let's use the time we have well.

There are few things that will help you appreciate the speed of time like noticing how quickly your children are growing up. Don't waste your time on things that don't matter! Spend your moments like valuable currency. Invest in your kids' lives. Talk to them. Play with them. Read to them. Ask them questions.

There are twenty-four hours today that you'll never get back. In truth, you don't even know if you've got that. How are you going to spend your time wisely with your kids?

PRAY:

Lord, help me value each moment I have with my kids. Keep me from wasting time on sinful pursuits. When I mess up, make my heart burn until I'm right with You. Amen.

BE HOSPITABLE

Read 3 John 1

KEY VERSES:

Beloved, it is a faithful thing you do in all your efforts for these brothers, strangers as they are, who testified to your love before the church. You will do well to send them on their journey in a manner worthy of God.

3 John 1:5–6 ESV

UNDERSTAND:

John wrote in today's passage that he has no greater joy than to hear that his children are walking in the truth. How do you walk in the truth?

....

....

....

....

....

Diotrephes was a member of the church, but he acted in self-focused ways, not caring for the needs of traveling missionaries. There are still self-focused people in the church today. How can you lovingly set them straight? Do you need to be set straight yourself?

....

....

....

....

....

....

APPLY:

"A man's home is his castle." That's how the saying goes, and it's true if you recognize where your true home is. For Christians, our "castle" can be found with God on the throne after this life is over. At best, the place we live right now is like a "home away from home."

Why is that important?

If you are too tied to the physical property of this earth, you will act in inhospitable ways. When people come over, do you invite them to treat your home like their own? Or do you enforce a "no shoes on the carpeting" rule and serve only water because anything else might stain the upholstery? Are you hospitable with your own kids, for that matter?

This world won't last. Our carpets and sofas won't either. It's time to use our temporary homes to further the eternal mission of sharing God's love.

PRAY:

Lord, give me a proper perspective on the things I consider mine. Everything is yours, both in this world and in the next. Help me appreciate people more than things. Give me a heart that sees beyond carpet stains to the mission of Your gospel. Amen.

BE SHAMELESS IN YOUR JOY

Read 2 Samuel 6

KEY VERSE:

Wearing a linen ephod, David was dancing before the LORD with all his might.

2 SAMUEL 6:14 NIV

UNDERSTAND:

Shortly after David was anointed king over Israel, he sought to restore the ark of the covenant to its home in Jerusalem. How do his actions indicate that he will be a different kind of king than his predecessor, Saul?

As David saw with Obed-Edom's household, God's presence and blessing could be found where the ark was. How is the ark of the covenant like your heart today?

APPLY:

When David assumed kingship over Israel, it was a long time coming. He had been anointed as the next king when he was a shepherd boy too small to be considered among his older brothers (see 1 Samuel 16:1–13). By the time he was proclaimed king of Israel, David was due for some kingly rest and relaxation.

But that's not what he did. Why not? David knew that he wasn't truly the king of Israel. God was.

David went to retrieve the ark of the covenant—the place where God's presence was known to be. He organized his own coronation procession with troops and trumpets. He stripped off his royal garments and joined the priests in their simple linens, praising along with the rest that God was taking His rightful place at the heart of Israel.

David danced with joy because he felt the presence of the Lord. Are you dancing today? Or are you judging those who do?

PRAY:

Father God, I don't need to have the ark of the covenant in my home to know that You are with me. May others see the blessing of Your presence in my life and desire it for themselves. Help my kids see the joy that Your presence brings, and let me express that joy without shame. Amen.

BE CAREFUL HOW YOU CORRECT

Read Matthew 18:10–35

KEY VERSE:

"If your brother sins against you, go and tell him his fault, between you and him alone. If he listens to you, you have gained your brother."
MATTHEW 18:15 ESV

UNDERSTAND:

How do the parable of the lost sheep (verses 10–14) and the advice on how to address sin between believers (verses 15–20) express the importance of restoring broken relationships?

How does the concept of forgiveness (verses 21–35) play into restoring relationships?

Why is it better to address sin one-on-one before bringing more people into the situation?

APPLY:

One of the most difficult parts of parenting is handling corrections. Thinking up punishments to fit crimes requires thoroughly understanding what motivated our kids to disobey us in the first place. Restoring broken relationships can be emotionally draining. And how we handle ourselves will affect how our kids see God the Father as either a mean punisher of sins or as a loving force for restoration.

So yeah, parenting is hard.

Fortunately, God gave us some advice in today's passage. Remember that the goal of all correction is to restore a broken relationship. That's not going to happen when we embarrass our kids in front of their siblings or friends. Restoration should start with a calm one-on-one conversation. If the offense you're addressing has you still fuming with anger, wait to address it until you are calm.

Also remember that forgiveness is a necessary skill for parents—for all believers—because God the Father has forgiven us.

....

....

....

....

....

....

....

....

PRAY:

Lord, when You correct me, it is to restore me to a right relationship with You. There is no shame in Your love. Help me to correct my children in the same way, forgiving always and treating them with the respect You show me. Amen.

PLAY BY THE RULES

Read Exodus 20:1–21

KEY VERSES:

I am the LORD thy God, which have brought thee out of the land of Egypt, out of the house of bondage. Thou shalt have no other gods before me.

EXODUS 20:2–3 KJV

UNDERSTAND:

The first half of the Ten Commandments are about how we relate to God. The second half are about how we relate to each other. Which commandments do you struggle with most?

....

....

....

....

....

How would you react if you were in the crowd at the bottom of the mountain while God spoke audibly to His people? How do you listen to Him now?

....

....

....

....

....

....

APPLY:

All games have rules. If you violate the rules, the game isn't fun and the other players get mad. The rules exist to establish order, to keep people safe, and to keep things from descending into chaos. Your relationship with God isn't a game, but the rules He laid out in today's passage were given for similar reasons.

God loves His people. Before any of the commandments are given, He reminds them of who He is and what He's done for them. God brought them out of slavery to make them His holy nation. And because He loves them, He wants them to live according to a set of guidelines that will keep them safe and able to stay close to Him without the need for correction.

Whenever you play a game with your kids, remember why the rules exist, and tell your kids about God's rules for living well. Make sure you are following them yourself!

PRAY:

God, You have brought me out of slavery to sin and set me apart for You. Help me play by the rules You've laid out. I know they exist for my good and for Your glory. May my children see rule following not as a limit on freedom but as an expression of love. Amen.

SAY "I LOVE YOU"

Read John 13:1–35

KEY VERSES:

A new commandment I give unto you, That ye love one another; as I have loved you, that ye also love one another. By this shall all men know that ye are my disciples, if ye have love one to another.

John 13:34–35 KJV

UNDERSTAND:

John 13:1 (KJV) describes Jesus as "having loved his own which were in the world, he loved them unto the end." How can you love your own kids "unto the end"?

....

....

....

Why is it significant that Jesus washed His disciples' feet?

....

....

....

....

Do people know you are a disciple of Jesus by the way you show love?

....

....

....

....

APPLY:

In all relationships, we are either in the process of turning toward someone or turning away from them. When we turn toward them, the person feels our support, our attention, and our love. Emotionally healthy relationships are characterized by this turning toward each other, and saying "I love you" aloud is an important part of turning toward our children.

But there's a catch.

If the words are only words, don't say them. If you say, "I love you," while turning your attention away from them, they'll come to associate your "love" with apathy and lose trust in what you say.

In today's passage, Jesus verbally told His disciples He loved them. He commanded them to love each other. He showed them an example of love by serving them through foot washing. Today, tell your kids you love them, but back it up with action too.

....

....

....

....

....

....

....

....

....

PRAY:

Jesus, You've loved me from before I was born. You expressed it most deeply when You died for my sins. May I die to my sin today and put the interests of others ahead of my own. Help me verbalize my love for my kids in ways that they understand. Amen.

PRAISE GOD IN NATURE

Read Psalm 145

KEY VERSE:

On the glorious splendor of your majesty,
and on your wondrous works, I will meditate.
PSALM 145:5 ESV

UNDERSTAND:

Today's passage uses many different words for praising God. Make a list of all the examples you can find. Why do you think David used so many different words for praise?

....

....

....

Verses 10–12 say all the saints shall bless God and make known to their children His mighty deeds. How have you shared God's deeds to your kids?

....

....

....

Verses 15–16 speak of God's providence toward every living thing. How has God provided for you?

....

....

....

....

APPLY:

Psalm 145 is the final recorded psalm of David. It is filled with reasons to praise God—His goodness, righteousness, mighty deeds, and generosity among them.

One place we can appreciate the splendor of God's majesty is in nature. As the Creator of something as large as the cosmos, God paid special attention to the smallest details of creation. He designed trees to grow seeds capable of self-replication. He designed creatures like sea anemones and hermit crabs to work together in symbiotic partnership. He designed vastly different environments for vastly different creatures; then He made mankind in His own image.

If you want to share some of God's splendor with your kids, take them on a hike in the world He created. Read up on some of the sights you expect to see and explain to your kids how God made everything unique and for His glory.

PRAY:

Creator God, You are endlessly creative. Thank You for making me in Your image so I can better appreciate the things You have made. You are generous, good, and kind. Help me make Your glory known to my children through my words and actions. Amen.

MODEL SELF-SACRIFICE

Read John 15

KEY VERSE:

"Greater love has no one than this:
to lay down one's life for one's friends."
JOHN 15:13 NIV

UNDERSTAND:

Grapevines are divided into multiple parts: roots, trunk, branches, leaves, and fruit. When Jesus said in today's passage that He is the true vine and we are the branches, what does that mean?

How is the fruit of self-sacrifice a natural outgrowth of Christ as the true vine?

How has God been pruning you so you'll bear more fruit?

APPLY:

When you became a dad, you probably noticed how helpless babies are. They can't feed themselves, clean themselves, or do anything, really. They are wholly dependent on others to care for their needs. So, what happened when your baby's needs conflicted with your own?

Hopefully, you are the type of dad who set his needs aside and pitched in. But there was still some part of you that wondered, *When will I get to sleep through the night again?* Laying down our lives for our kids might be a no-brainer for you, but what about dying to your desires for small things like watching what you want instead of whatever kids' show your child loves?

The hard part of modeling self-sacrifice is that it will go unnoticed 90 percent of the time, but when your kids do see it, they'll be more likely to do it too. Conversely, if you are selfish all the time, your kids will likely grow up to model your selfish behavior.

....

....

....

....

....

....

....

....

....

....

PRAY:

Lord, help me remain in Your love.
Remind me often that I'm not to live for myself.
Help my children see self-sacrifice as part of
what it means to bear spiritual fruit. Amen.

SEEK QUALITY ADVICE

Read Psalm 1:1–6

KEY VERSES:

Blessed is the man who walks not in the counsel of the wicked, nor stands in the way of sinners, nor sits in the seat of scoffers; but his delight is in the law of the LORD, *and on his law he meditates day and night.*

PSALM 1:1–2 ESV

UNDERSTAND:

Much has been made of the "walk, stand, sit" regression of movement when we listen to wicked advisors. How have you been tempted to slow down in your faith journey because of sin's allure?

Verses 3–4 contrast the permanency and usefulness of the faithful with the temporary and futile life of the wicked. How is the fruitfulness of faith evident in your parenting?

APPLY:

Whom do you go to for advice? This world has no shortage of folks offering answers to questions no one asked. We are constantly bombarded with marketing messages telling us to do what makes us happy, to have it our way, that we deserve better. The world appeals to our selfish nature and tells us that we are smart enough to decide what is right by us.

What does the Bible say? Proverbs 14:12 (ESV) says, "There is a way that seems right to a man, but its end is the way to death."

If we want to avoid the fate of the wicked and the ignorant, we need to know where to go for good advice. Proverbs 3:5–6 (ESV) says, "Trust in the LORD with all your heart, and do not lean on your own understanding. In all your ways acknowledge him, and he will make straight your paths."

PRAY:

Lord, when I have questions, keep me from seeking answers in the wrong places. Show me how to trust You more than my own understanding. When someone appeals to my selfish nature, help me realize where that path ends. Amen.

TAKE CARE OF YOUR BODY

Read 1 Corinthians 6

KEY VERSES:

Do you not know that your bodies are temples of the Holy Spirit, who is in you, whom you have received from God? You are not your own; you were bought at a price. Therefore honor God with your bodies.

1 Corinthians 6:19–20 NIV

UNDERSTAND:

How is the body of Christ—the church—like the individual body of a believer?

....

....

Verses 12–13 utilize some phrases that were probably common to the Corinthian believers. How are these phrases like ones you might hear in modern advertising?

....

....

....

What are some of the reasons given in today's passage to honor God with your body, both sexually and in other ways?

....

....

....

....

APPLY:

There are practical reasons to take care of your body: increased longevity, fewer medical bills, and being better able to keep up with your children. As you read in today's passage, there are spiritual reasons as well.

Much of today's passage is dedicated to the idea that a self-centered, "whatever feels good" mindset is incompatible with the influence of the Holy Spirit dwelling within us. Paul reminds his readers that although they may have once lived for the temporary pleasures of this world, they have been washed and sanctified by Jesus for better purposes (see verses 9–11).

So the next time you find yourself reaching for something that will only offer temporary pleasure, whether it's a bag of donuts or a website you know you shouldn't visit, think again. Remember that Christ bought you at a price and your body is the temple of the Holy Spirit.

PRAY:

Lord, I am Yours, in mind, body, and spirit. Help me live to honor and please You more than myself. May I look for ways to glorify You with my body. Keep me from taking pride in what You have created for Your own purposes. Amen.

LET YOUR KID DO THE PROJECT

Read 2 Timothy 2

KEY VERSE:

An athlete is not crowned unless he competes according to the rules.
2 Timothy 2:5 ESV

UNDERSTAND:

Suffering is part of the Christian experience, especially when you are living for Christ. Why is it important to suffer well?

Paul wrote to Timothy about suffering, duty, and hard work using examples of soldiers, athletes, and farmers. What kind of example do you set in your work?

How do you present yourself to God as one approved (see verses 15–19)?

APPLY:

From science projects to book reports to Pinewood Derby competitions, dads have a long history of doing their children's work for them. There's just something about vicariously winning a trophy that calls to us.

At first, we stand by as our kids brainstorm a plan for their project, but it doesn't take long for us to make a few suggestions on how they might do things better. From suggestion to "helping" them—by taking the project out of their hands and working on it ourselves—is a short trip indeed.

But that's not how the projects are supposed to be. Sure, kids can learn by watching us, but this is their project. The rules state that they need to do the thing themselves. And only by playing according to the rules will they possibly win. Or better yet, learn how to do things on their own.

....

....

....

....

....

....

....

....

....

PRAY:

Lord, keep my hands off the work You've reserved for someone else to accomplish. May I help without taking over and teach in the best way for others to learn. Help me suffer well if that's what it takes to play by the rules. Amen.

DROP YOUR KIDS AN ENCOURAGING NOTE

Read 1 Thessalonians 1

KEY VERSES:

We give thanks to God always for you all, making mention of you in our prayers; remembering without ceasing your work of faith, and labour of love, and patience of hope in our Lord Jesus Christ, in the sight of God and our Father.

1 Thessalonians 1:2–3 KJV

UNDERSTAND:

Thessalonica was the capital of Macedonia, a province of the Roman empire. Paul's letter to the Thessalonians is a follow-up to the church's founding (see Acts 17) and begins with prayers and praise. How can you share the gospel like Paul and minister to people at different stages in their faith?

....

....

How are your own children part of your ministry?

....

....

....

What are some ways you can encourage them to grow in their faith?

....

....

....

APPLY:

The church at Thessalonica was founded when Paul shared the gospel over three Sabbath days in the synagogue, making believers out of Jews and Greeks, women and men alike. There was a rocky period immediately afterward when Paul's host, Jason, was dragged from his home and basically robbed, but the church of God took root.

Paul's letter to the Thessalonians opens with warm encouragement. While things may not have started smoothly, the church overcame opposition and expanded throughout the region. Paul wanted to remind them that he was praying for them and that they were doing a great job.

Things in your household may be rocky from time to time, but you have a ministry there. Don't forget to encourage your family members by praying for them and telling them what they are doing well. In fact, why not write your kids a note today to tell them just that?

....

....

....

....

....

....

....

....

....

PRAY:

Father God, You are with me when things don't go according to my plan. Help me encourage my family as Paul encouraged the church at Thessalonica. May my kids have influence with their friends because I am sharing my faith with them. Amen.

READ THE BIBLE AS A FAMILY

Read John 1:1–34

KEY VERSE:

In the beginning was the Word, and the Word was with God, and the Word was God.

John 1:1 NIV

UNDERSTAND:

The beginning of John's gospel sounds a lot like the beginning of Genesis. In what ways are the two texts related?

John introduces his gospel by listing some of the themes he'll touch on later—Jesus is the light (verse 7) and the truth (verse 14). How have you proclaimed the attributes and identity of Jesus to those around you?

APPLY:

The Gospel of John uses more poetic language than Matthew, Mark, or Luke in referring to Jesus Christ. In fact, John's inclusion in the New Testament canon was debated for being so different from the other gospels. In the end, the early church fathers suggested that John was aware of the other gospels and added his own as a spiritual gospel.

It is good that he did. Can you imagine the Bible without John 3:16? Or today's verse? John sought to make Jesus known through words that were both poetic and true. In the beginning, God spoke creation into being through Jesus. Jesus literally was the Word.

The Bible too is the Word of God, and as a dad, you get to share Jesus with your kids in ways that they will understand. Start with a verse or two that means something special to you and share it with your kids. Read the Bible together. Start a family devotional. Be John and introduce them to the Word.

....

....

....

....

....

....

....

....

....

....

PRAY:

Jesus, help me faithfully present Your truth to my family. Help me show them that You are the light and the truth. May I start a practice in them that they'll continue long afterward. Amen.

REPEAT YOURSELF WITH LOVE

Read 1 Thessalonians 5

KEY VERSE:

And we urge you, brothers, admonish the idle, encourage the fainthearted, help the weak, be patient with them all.

1 Thessalonians 5:14 ESV

UNDERSTAND:

There was concern in the church of Thessalonica that people who died before Jesus' second coming would miss out on being reunited with Him. How does Paul address these concerns in today's passage?

....

....

....

....

....

....

The second half of today's passage includes a laundry list of spiritual advice. How might you work on memorizing verses 14–22?

....

....

....

....

....

....

APPLY:

If you've told them once, you've told them a thousand times: Put the dirty clothes in the hamper. Push in your chair. Turn off the light when you leave the room. Wash your hands. You can fill in the rest of the list.

Why is it so hard for kids to remember?

Paul might wonder the same thing about us. In his letter to the Thessalonians, Paul includes a list of reminders before signing off: "Rejoice always, pray without ceasing, give thanks in all circumstances; for this is the will of God in Christ Jesus for you. Do not quench the Spirit. Do not despise prophecies, but test everything; hold fast what is good. Abstain from every form of evil" (1 Thessalonians 5:16–22 ESV).

These rapid-fire reminders for Christians were given with love, not exasperation, and they can serve as a model for how you are to approach your kids. Remind them of the important things often, but do so in love.

PRAY:

Lord, You are patient with me. Help me be patient with my kids. You lovingly remind me of what is important. May I show the same respect to my children. Forgive me when I allow my frustrations to get in the way of Your love. Amen.

EMBRACE THE GIFT OF WORK

Read Genesis 2

KEY VERSE:

The Lord God took the man and put him in the Garden of Eden to work it and take care of it.
Genesis 2:15 NIV

UNDERSTAND:

Today's passage is a more intimate account of God's creation of mankind. What examples in the text point to God's loving nature as He created Adam and Eve?

....

....

....

....

....

....

Before God put Adam in the Garden of Eden to work it and care for it, God was responsible for that job. What is the relationship between sharing in God's image and sharing in God's responsibilities?

....

....

....

....

....

....

APPLY:

Some people picture the perfect afterlife as lounging on clouds, lazily strumming on harps, and relaxing with whatever heavenly beverages are close at hand. There are problems with this view, however. First, this image of the afterlife comes from pop culture, not the Bible. Second, the idea of lazily doing nothing except satisfying our earthly desires runs counter to how we were created to be.

Believe it or not, work—not the lack of responsibility—is a gift from God. Before Adam and Eve ate the forbidden fruit, God gave Adam a job to do. Sure, sinfulness made his job harder—the thorns of the ground were a result of mankind's sin—but the job itself was a blessing.

Why? Because God is a doer. It's one of the first thing we learn about Him in the Bible. And when He made us in His image, He made us to be doers too.

....

....

....

....

....

....

....

....

....

PRAY:

Father God, thank You for the gift of work. Help me see it as a gift instead of a curse. Correct my vision of what a perfect afterlife looks like. May I appreciate the gift of work now so my kids can see that by working, I am sharing in Your image. Amen.

MANAGE WELL

Read 1 Timothy 3

KEY VERSE:

He must manage his own family well and see that his children obey him, and he must do so in a manner worthy of full respect.

1 Timothy 3:4 NIV

UNDERSTAND:

Today's passage outlines some character traits of men who would serve well in the offices of church leadership, but the same traits are desirable for all men. Why is it important that the leaders of the church manage their own houses well?

....

....

....

Why do you think verse 6 advises that recent converts to Christianity take time to mature before serving in a leadership capacity?

....

....

....

Which character traits could you use some spiritual help in growing?

....

....

....

....

APPLY:

According to *Entrepreneur* magazine, the "10 Golden Rules of Effective Management" include: be consistent, be the example, publicly reward and recognize hard work, encourage all opinions and ideas, and listen and ask questions, among others.

When it comes to managing your household, these same rules apply. While some guys read today's verse as a justification to be the tyrant in their own home, micromanaging what everyone is allowed to say and do, good management doesn't work like that.

To manage your household, you need to show that you care about the people you lead. You need to lay down what you want and set an example of self-sacrifice. You need to listen more often than you speak, be consistent in your godly walk, and recognize the strengths of everyone. Don't fall into the trap that a man's role is in one area and a wife's is in another if you are each better suited to non-stereotypical roles.

Above all else, look to God's example of leadership and follow suit.

PRAY:

Jesus, You inspired others with truth and love.
May I lead like You and manage my household
in the same way You manage Yours. Amen.

TELL STORIES

Read Matthew 13:1–23

KEY VERSES:

Then the disciples came and said to him, "Why do you speak to them in parables?" And he answered them, "To you it has been given to know the secrets of the kingdom of heaven, but to them it has not been given."
MATTHEW 13:10–11 ESV

UNDERSTAND:

The first parable in Matthew 13—a chapter sometimes called the Parabolic Discourse—is about the different kinds of listeners to the message of God's kingdom. Why do you think Jesus started His discourse about people who listen?

....

....

....

What makes the "good soil" in the parable of the sower "good"?

....

....

....

How can you improve the quality of your soil in ways your children can see?

....

....

....

APPLY:

Everyone loves a good story. From books to movies to television shows to friends who share what they did over the weekend, we are drawn to connection with others through stories. Their universal appeal was surely one aspect of Jesus' use of stories when teaching the multitudes. His audience didn't always understand the thrust of His stories—that's the other reason He taught in parables—but they listened to Jesus all the same.

Kids are a prime audience for stories. When they might otherwise be bouncing off the walls, when you start to tell a story, they'll stop for a minute to listen. Need to hone your storytelling skills? Start with books you enjoyed when you were young. Establish the practice of reading together. Introduce them to Bible stories and start turning over the soil of their hearts so they can listen for God's voice hidden behind your own.

Share in the fact that you are part of God's story of redemption!

PRAY:

Lord, You taught in stories to reach people in the ways You knew they needed. Help me share stories with my kids that show them their need for You. Help me to listen to Your story for me. Amen.

LIVE UNDER GRACE

Read Romans 6

KEY VERSE:

For sin shall not have dominion over you:
for ye are not under the law, but under grace.
ROMANS 6:14 KJV

UNDERSTAND:

Paul, before his conversion to Christianity, was a zealous adherent to the Hebrew law. He ate, slept, and breathed the law. Consider the significance of the source, then, who is telling us that we are no longer under the law but under grace.

What does it mean to you to be dead to sin and alive to God in Jesus?

What is different between life under the law versus life under grace when you mess up?

APPLY:

When you accumulate a monetary debt in this world, you must pay it off—often with interest. Debts have a way of following you through life. Even loan forgiveness programs have certain requirements that people have to qualify for and follow.

But grace and spiritual debts work on a different system entirely. Jesus assumed our debts on the cross. He paid them and continues to pay them for the entirety of our lives. Under the law, each sin had to be accounted for individually, and sacrifices needed to be made for every offense. When grace came in, the old system under the law ended because Jesus was the perfect sacrifice.

Live today under grace, not cowering under old debts that don't belong to you but praising God for every blessing you've received. You can't do more than Jesus already did, so accept forgiveness and move on.

PRAY:

Jesus, Your sacrifice on the cross was enough. Help me to not wallow in past mistakes but live confidently in Your present victory. Thank You for paying my debts and calling me Your own. Amen.

TEACH AS ONE WHO IS TAUGHT

Read Isaiah 50:4–51:8

KEY VERSE:

The Lord God has given me the tongue of those who are taught, that I may know how to sustain with a word him who is weary. Morning by morning he awakens; he awakens my ear to hear as those who are taught.

Isaiah 50:4 ESV

UNDERSTAND:

Today's passage is an Old Testament anticipation of the Messiah. Which verses stood out to you as familiar because of things Jesus said?

Phrases like "Listen to me" and "Give attention to me" are sprinkled throughout today's reading. How are you listening to God in your life?

How are you teaching others from a place of humility?

APPLY:

God is all-knowing, but He takes time to listen. Think about that. God already knows what you need better than you know what to ask for, but He encourages us to pray. He has written the end of the story in His Word, but He longs to be close to you in the middle of your conflict. He teaches from a place of humility, even though He knows every aspect of the subject matter.

Now think about a teacher who *thinks* he knows everything. Teachers like that are insufferable! They don't listen to their students. They don't care about their contributions. They don't attempt to learn at all.

As you raise your children, you'll naturally know more than they do, but think about what kind of teacher you want to be, what kind of teacher they will listen to. If Jesus can teach as one who is taught, even though He knows everything, you can too.

PRAY:

Lord, help me listen so I can teach. Help me teach as one who is taught. Keep me from acting like a know-it-all. May I model a humble and teachable spirit for my kids. Amen.

MAKE SOMETHING TOGETHER

Read Genesis 1

KEY VERSE:

And God saw everything that he had made, and behold, it was very good. And there was evening and there was morning, the sixth day.

Genesis 1:31 ESV

UNDERSTAND:

Creativity is often a chaotic process, but God imposes order throughout the creation narrative. What are some instances of this ordering of creation in the text?

....

....

....

The text of verse 26 quotes God addressing a plural audience, which many scholars believe to be the earliest reference to God's triune nature—Father, Son, and Holy Spirit. Why does creativity often work best when more than one person is involved?

....

....

....

What are some creative pursuits you can tackle with your kids?

....

....

....

APPLY:

Have you ever said, "I'm just not the creative type," when someone asks for help with a project? While it may be true that you aren't the next Leonardo da Vinci, it is also true that you were created in the image of God (see verse 27 in today's text) and that God is *definitely* creative. It's literally the first thing we find out about Him!

In order to better understand the God we serve, it is good to be like Him in His creativity. Even better, it is good to be like Him in inviting your kids to be part of the process.

It doesn't matter if you can't color without your crayons slipping out of the lines or if no one can tell what your playdough sculpture is supposed to be. You don't have to be the best at something to get the benefits of time together or an appreciation of how difficult artistic pursuits can be. Go make something and praise God for the way He's made you in His image!

....

....

....

....

....

....

....

....

....

PRAY:

God, everything You've made is amazing and good. I can't compete with You, but I can praise You better by understanding the care and order that goes into creative pursuits. Help me show my children the value of all forms of creativity. Amen.

LET YOUR KIDS BE THEMSELVES

Read 1 Corinthians 12

KEY VERSE:

For the body is not one member, but many.
1 Corinthians 12:14 KJV

UNDERSTAND:

First Corinthians 12 says that all believers are given spiritual gifts. What things on the list of mentioned gifts are you naturally drawn toward?

How might you use your gifts to bless others?

What gifts do you see in your children that you might nurture into greater prominence in their lives?

APPLY:

It's easy to look at your kids when they do something just like you and think that they are miniature versions of yourself. Some parents, consciously or subconsciously, raise their kids to be just that. The problem is that your kids are not designed to be a miniature version of you. They might look like you and say things they hear you say, but they are designed by God to be fully themselves.

It's good to realize that before you judge them too harshly for doing things you wouldn't do, for being drawn toward things you do not care for, or for following pursuits you wouldn't have chosen for yourself. As you read today's passage, did you think about how you might be an eye in the body of Christ and your child might be an ear?

Love your kids for who they are. Raise them to be sufficient like you but in their own ways. Trust them to God.

PRAY:

Lord, help me recognize when I'm trying to turn my kids into me. Help me develop them to be more like You. I trust You with my children's future and want to do my best with their present. Amen.

PROTECT YOUR KIDS AS GOD WOULD

Read Psalm 91

KEY VERSE:

"Because he loves me," says the LORD, "I will rescue him; I will protect him, for he acknowledges my name."
PSALM 91:14 NIV

UNDERSTAND:

Psalm 91 spells out several dangers encountered by the psalmist—hidden traps, deadly diseases, night terrors, and daytime arrows—all of which he is protected from by God's deliverance. What dangers do you face today?

Does your faith depend on whether God protects you from all harm?

How might your faith grow when you remember God's promises in the midst of danger?

APPLY:

Babies are helpless. This isn't a judgment on babies. No one expects them to come into the world as self-defense experts. Even eighteen-year-olds aren't fully equipped to deal with the dangers of the world, even if the world calls them adults. The areas of their brain that process dangerous situations and come up with well-thought-out solutions aren't fully connected yet!

That's where you come in. As the grown-up in this situation, you are responsible for protecting your kids from danger. Sometimes this means allowing them to make mistakes so they can learn from the consequences of their actions. Shielding them from all harm turns kids into foolhardy people. Maybe that's why God allows us to experience danger too—so we can learn from our mistakes and better trust Him with our futures.

Be the shield for your kids, but even better, help them know where their safety is most sure: trusting in God's plan for their lives, no matter the dangers they'll face.

....

....

....

....

....

....

....

PRAY:

Father God, give me wisdom to protect my kids from harm, even when that means allowing them to be in danger. Help me trust in Your plan more than my own. You will keep me safe from any harm that threatens my faith in You. Amen.

TRY FASTING

Read Matthew 6:1–18

KEY VERSES:

"But when you fast, anoint your head and wash your face, that your fasting may not be seen by others but by your Father who is in secret. And your Father who sees in secret will reward you."
MATTHEW 6:17–18 ESV

UNDERSTAND:

Genuine faith doesn't seek the attention of others. In today's passage, Jesus identifies some different ways people act hypocritically in the practices of their faith. What are some others you can think of?

....

....

....

....

....

Jesus isn't suggesting that all public forms of caring for the poor, prayer, and fasting are wrong, but He's saying that when they are done for the wrong reasons, they aren't further rewarded. What are your motivations when living out your faith publicly?

....

....

....

....

....

APPLY:

What is fasting? It's giving something up for a specific time frame to express commitment to God and to strengthen your prayer life.

Fasting isn't as popular as some other faith practices. There are about seven times more books on prayer than on fasting. People understand the need for prayer because it's how we ask God for things (FYI—prayer is a lot more than just asking God for things). Social media enables people to donate to the needy with the click of a button, then shares that you donated with your friends. But fasting isn't something you share for social media credit (FYI—donating to the needy shouldn't be either).

So why fast? Because it sharpens your faith. If you give up all beverages other than water, each time you find yourself craving coffee or soda, you'll be reminded of your fast and will pray instead. Do it privately. Take the opportunity to pray for your kids. Realize that your need for God is greater than your need for coffee or soda.

PRAY:

Lord, prayer and helping the needy take time, but they don't cause discomfort in the same personal way as fasting. Help my commitment to You to be stronger than my commitment to anything else. May I fast for the right reasons and honor You in the process. Amen.

BE FILLED WITH THE RIGHT THINGS

Read Philippians 4

KEY VERSE:

Finally, brothers and sisters, whatever is true, whatever is noble, whatever is right, whatever is pure, whatever is lovely, whatever is admirable—if anything is excellent or praiseworthy—think about such things.

PHILIPPIANS 4:8 NIV

UNDERSTAND:

In Philippians 4, Paul addresses the need for reconciliation, rejoicing, and relying on God's provision. According to the text, what things lead to the peace of God?

....

....

....

Philippians 4:13 is an oft-quoted but misunderstood verse. How does it apply in the context of scarcity and contentment?

....

....

....

Do you feel the peace of God in your life?

....

....

....

APPLY:

Like a tube of toothpaste, our lives will show what we're filled with when we get squeezed. If we're filled with bitterness, doubt, and selfishness, it'll come out when the pressures of the world press down on us. If we're prayerful with our concerns, thankful for God's provision, and thinking about true, noble, and lovely things, that'll come out instead.

Our thoughts will direct our actions. After advising his readers to think on praiseworthy things (see today's verse), Paul writes, "Whatever you have learned or received or heard from me, or seen in me—put it into practice. And the God of peace will be with you" (Philippians 4:9 NIV). We can't let our good thoughts stagnate; we are to put them into practice.

Take some time to examine your thoughts. Do you find yourself dwelling on godly things or selfish things? Bring all your thoughts under submission with help from the Holy Spirit.

PRAY:

Lord, You give me so many good things to think about. Turn my mind toward You. Thank You for the blessings You've given me as a dad. When I'm squeezed by life, may my kids see that what comes out is honoring to You. Amen.

BUILD A FORT TOGETHER

Read Matthew 7

KEY VERSE:

"Everyone then who hears these words of mine and does them will be like a wise man who built his house on the rock."

MATTHEW 7:24 ESV

UNDERSTAND:

Today's passage is full of phrases and stories that are familiar, even in pop culture, but their messages may be degraded by their familiarity. Ask God to show you this important section of scripture with fresh eyes.

....

....

....

In many ways, Jesus is drawing a line in the sand with the religious elites of His day. Listeners can either follow Him or turn away. How is that presented in the text?

....

....

....

What is the foundation of your faith?

....

....

....

....

APPLY:

If you've ever built a blanket fort with your kids, you know there are right ways (and wrong ways) to build it. Some dads use clothespins to secure blankets in place. Others use heavy books to keep them from shifting. In the end, if the blanket fort stands against the storms of playtime that happen within it, it was a fort well built.

In today's passage, Jesus talks about the difference between a life built on a solid foundation and one built on sand. In the hot summer months around the Sea of Galilee, where Jesus is preaching in the passage, the sand dries out and hardens. It certainly looks like a good surface to build on. But when the rainy season hits, anything built on that sand will wash away.

Mention this parable the next time you build a fort with your kids. Help them see the wisdom of building a faith to stand, even in the toughest of storms.

PRAY:

Jesus, You are the solid foundation on which my faith is built. Anything else will wash away. Help me always choose the right side of the line that You drew in the sand. Amen.

KEEP YOUR COMMITMENTS

Read Ecclesiastes 5

KEY VERSES:

When you make a vow to God, do not delay to fulfill it. He has no pleasure in fools; fulfill your vow. It is better not to make a vow than to make one and not fulfill it.

ECCLESIASTES 5:4–5 NIV

UNDERSTAND:

If sacrifices didn't require much from us, they wouldn't be sacrifices. Today's passage includes instructions for those who promise a sacrifice in exchange for help from God in some way. Have you ever promised God something in exchange for His help?

....

....

....

....

....

Ecclesiastes 5 also portrays the folly of a man who works hard his whole life, then loses his riches on a bad investment. What's worse is that he has a family who depends on him. How can you avoid this fate?

....

....

....

....

....

....

APPLY:

There is no better way to lose trust with your kids than to make a promise and not keep it. If you promise to be at their school play, dance recital, or sporting event, you'd better show up. When you follow through on your word, you build trust. When you don't, the relationship between you suffers.

That's why it's also a big deal when we break our vows to God. If we promise God something one moment, then break the promise the next, we damage the relationship between us. God isn't harmed by our broken promise, but we are less likely to go to Him when we need Him in the future. Our shame will keep us distant.

With our kids and God, it is best to be men of our word, proving trustworthy to keep our commitments whenever we make them.

....

....

....

....

....

....

....

....

....

....

PRAY:

Father, forgive me for the times when I've proven untrustworthy with You. Help me fulfill my promises to You and to my children. I want them to trust me so that when I talk about You, they can know that what I'm saying is real. Amen.

BE RESILIENT

Read Isaiah 41:1–20

KEY VERSE:

Fear thou not; for I am with thee: be not dismayed; for I am thy God: I will strengthen thee; yea, I will help thee; yea, I will uphold thee with the right hand of my righteousness.

Isaiah 41:10 KJV

UNDERSTAND:

Isaiah 41 is a challenge by God to the nations that want to rewrite history without Israel in it. How does God reassure Israel amid their hardship?

....

....

....

In verse 14, God refers to Israel as a worm—an animal not known for its fierce teeth. What does God compare them to when He strengthens them?

....

....

....

How does God promise to care for the oppressed?

....

....

....

APPLY:

Resilience is the ability to bounce back from trials. Throughout the Old Testament, God helped Israel bounce back whenever they turned toward Him for assistance. Without God's help, they were helpless against invaders, but with God, they had nothing to worry about.

You might be facing some trials right now. Whether problems at work, miscommunications with your wife, or the kids are pushing your buttons, God's message to Israel from today's passage applies to you too.

God chose you to be His own. He has gathered you to Himself. You have nothing to fear. God is with you. He will keep hold of you with His righteous right hand. Although you're only as fierce as a worm, He will turn you into a threshing sledge. When you are thirsty, He will refresh you with living water.

Don't let your trials get you down. Turn to God and thank Him for choosing you!

....

....

....

....

....

....

....

....

....

PRAY:

Father God, You are there for me in every trial.
I won't be overcome when I live in Your strength.
Strengthen me against every agitation I face.
Thank You for choosing me to be Your servant. Amen.

LEAVE ANGER AT THE DOOR

Read Psalm 37

KEY VERSE:

Refrain from anger, and forsake wrath!
Fret not yourself; it tends only to evil.
Psalm 37:8 ESV

UNDERSTAND:

Psalm 37 revolves around the destinies of the wicked and the righteous. Why did the author write this psalm?

....

....

....

....

How does a proper understanding of the limited benefits of wickedness help you choose to live righteously?

....

....

....

....

How can you demonstrate your reliance on God's justice and timing, even when you see the wicked prevailing today?

....

....

....

....

APPLY:

Look around and you'll see that the world is a broken place. People with power use it to stay in power. The rich get richer, and the poor get poorer. Violence against minority groups is on the rise. And that's just the big, newsworthy stuff. You can probably name ways the world is broken in your workplace, community, and maybe even your church too.

Here's what you need to know to succeed: This broken world is temporary. The wicked will not always prosper. God's justice will prevail.

It's easy to get angry when we experience the world's brokenness. But anger will only make more anger. Instead, we are called to forsake anger and embrace righteousness.

When you've had a hard day at work, drop your anger at the door. Thank God for your family. Combat your anger with gratitude and help grow the right things in your kids—and in yourself.

PRAY:

Lord of peace, may I choose gratitude over anger and wait patiently while Your plans for restoration unfold against the brokenness and wickedness of the world. May my example lessen the anger in my household and raise the level of gratitude to You. Amen.

KNOW WHERE YOUR TREASURE IS

Read Matthew 6:19–34

KEY VERSE:

For where your treasure is,
there will your heart be also.
MATTHEW 6:21 KJV

UNDERSTAND:

What does today's passage teach about the topic of riches and ownership?

How are your needs being met in ways that don't rely on money?

How does worrying about your concerns reveal your current level of trust in God?

APPLY:

The American dream of health, wealth, and a happy family isn't bad, per se. But is it good? Is it biblical? Is it God's intention to allow individuals to amass wealth for themselves at the cost of other people? To care for the physical needs of their families while ignoring the needs of those outside? Is God pleased when your family lives in happy ignorance while others suffer for lack of attention?

Obviously, when the American dream is held as a gospel truth, it can inspire some behaviors that conflict with God's priorities. To correct this view, we need to understand the point of money.

Money doesn't buy security, even if it feels like it does. It exists for us to show the world what is truly important. Does the way you spend money show the world where your riches truly lie? Pray today that God would show you where your treasure is and how to better use your riches for His glory.

PRAY:

Giver of all good things, You care for the flowers of the field and the birds of the air, so I know You care for me. Open my eyes to the ways I rely on money when I should be relying on You. Help me use the riches You've given to me to further Your message instead of my family's comfort. Amen.

HAVE A FAMILY MISSION STATEMENT

Read Joshua 24:1–18

KEY VERSE:

"And if it is evil in your eyes to serve the LORD, choose this day whom you will serve, whether the gods your fathers served in the region beyond the River, or the gods of the Amorites in whose land you dwell. But as for me and my house, we will serve the LORD."

JOSHUA 24:15 ESV

UNDERSTAND:

In today's passage, Joshua tells the story of Israel's history, from God's promise to Abraham to His defeat of the Amorites as Israel pushes toward the Promised Land. How do past victories inspire future faithfulness?

....

....

What is your history with God?

....

....

....

What is your family's spiritual mission statement?

....

....

....

APPLY:

After Moses died, Joshua led the children of Israel into the Promised Land. He was a skilled warrior, a gifted speaker, and a man of conviction. As he approached the end of his life, Joshua wanted the people of Israel to know their options and recommit to serving God.

Since Abraham was called from beyond the Euphrates, Joshua says the people could return to those gods. Or since they had just defeated the Amorites, they might consider serving their gods. But Joshua isn't interested in serving antique gods who mean nothing to him or gods who offer up their people for defeat. He will serve the one true God.

As Joshua made it clear to the people of Israel, you can make it clear to your family and community whom you serve. God has been faithful to you in the past, choosing you to follow Him, fighting on your behalf, and desiring a close relationship. Will you remain faithful to Him?

PRAY:

Father, thank You for choosing me to follow You. Thank You for going before me and clearing the path to the Promised Land of salvation. May I remain as faithful to You as You have been to me. Help me serve You well, because I can't do it on my own. Amen.

DON'T PUNISH WHILE YOU'RE ANGRY

Read Colossians 3:16–4:6

KEY VERSE:

Fathers, do not provoke your children,
lest they become discouraged.
COLOSSIANS 3:21 ESV

UNDERSTAND:

In addition to reading the Bible, how might you "let the word of Christ dwell in you richly" (Colossians 3:16 ESV)?

....

....

....

Paul addresses each member of the typical Roman household in Colossians 3:18–4:1. How do these instructions encourage kindness, love, and maintaining a witness for Christ?

....

....

....

How might you make sure that you are ready to answer questions about your faith?

....

....

....

....

APPLY:

Have you ever been angry with your kids? Of course you have! Kids do stuff to anger parents all the time. It's almost like their brains aren't working at full capacity yet (spoiler alert: They aren't).

There's nothing wrong with being angry when your kids do something monumentally unwise if you know how unwise it would be to punish them while you are still angry. To lash out against your kids in anger is incompatible with the love of Christ. Instead, take a minute to breathe. Pray for wisdom to address the situation. Think about how God has been good to you when you haven't deserved it. Then talk to your kids.

Your responsibility as a dad is to make sure your kids will know and love God. A lot of what they know about Him is gleaned by watching you. Don't let your anger get in the way of your testimony.

....

....

....

....

....

....

....

....

....

....

PRAY:

Father God, You have been good to me in spite of the unwise things I've done. Help me handle each situation with wisdom, grace, and justice. May my actions reflect Your love so my kids will know and trust You. Amen.

PRAISE WHAT IS PRAISEWORTHY

Read Matthew 25:1–30

KEY VERSE:

"His master said to him, 'Well done, good and faithful servant. You have been faithful over a little; I will set you over much. Enter into the joy of your master.'"

MATTHEW 25:21 ESV

UNDERSTAND:

How do the two parables from today's passage address how Christians should live when they don't know when Christ will return?

....

....

....

In the parable of the talents, each servant was given a different number of talents. A talent was equivalent to twenty years' wages. Why is it significant that the servant who made two talents for his master received the same praise as the one who earned five?

....

....

....

How are you using your resources to grow God's influence?

....

....

....

....

APPLY:

Praise God that our kids don't just make us angry. Our kids do wonderful things!

- They take joy in creation. You've probably got a pile of drawings they've made just for you stashed somewhere.
- They freely show their affection. Whether hugs and snuggles or playful roughhousing, our kids break down our emotional barriers with their physical expressions of love.
- They are kind and helpful. Sure, sometimes it can be a struggle to get your kids to do what they need to do, but just as often they will look for ways to help around the house.

You can surely think of other ways your kids are amazing, but do they know what you think of them? Take time today to praise those things that are praiseworthy. When you reinforce good behavior, they'll be more likely to repeat it in the future. If they think you don't care, they might try other—less healthy—ways to get your attention.

Go say, "Well done," and give them a hug!

PRAY:

Lord, You reward good behavior. Help me encourage my kids and notice the things worth praising. You've entrusted me with children, and they are worth more than all the talents in the world. May I raise them in such a way that You'll tell me, "Well done." Amen.

SPEND ONE-ON-ONE TIME WITH YOUR KIDS

Read Luke 5:1–26

KEY VERSES:

Yet the news about him spread all the more, so that crowds of people came to hear him and to be healed of their sicknesses. But Jesus often withdrew to lonely places and prayed.

Luke 5:15–16 NIV

UNDERSTAND:

Prior to becoming Jesus' disciple, Peter was a career fisherman. What do you think he was thinking when Jesus told him to row out into the deep waters and let his nets down after Peter had already had a disappointing night of fishing?

....

....

....

....

....

When fishing for fish or fishing for men, who provides the catch?

....

....

....

....

....

APPLY:

As Jesus performed miracles and taught people about God in authoritative, new ways, He naturally grew in popularity. One story from today's passage tells how Jesus boarded a boat to teach from the water because so many people were crowding around Him on the shore. Another story tells about a time when the house Jesus was in was so crowded that a group of men cut a hole in the roof so they could lower their paralytic friend inside for healing.

Everywhere He went, Jesus would have found crowds ready to listen and people ready to be healed, but He still made time to be alone with His Father in prayer.

Life is busy. Between your work schedule and your family's constant activities—not to mention any personal interests you have—who has time to add more things? Is it really that important to spend one-on-one time with your kids?

It was important to Jesus. How can you make time in your schedule to show your kids they are important to you?

....

....

....

....

....

....

....

PRAY:

Jesus, You made time for prayer when You were surrounded by people who needed You. Help me know what is most important and spend my time on things that matter. Make my prayer life echo Yours, and help my kids know that I love them. Open my schedule so I have time to spend one-on-one with them. Amen.

PROTECT YOUR CHILDREN'S INNOCENCE

Read 1 Corinthians 10

KEY VERSE:

There hath no temptation taken you but such as is common to man: but God is faithful, who will not suffer you to be tempted above that ye are able; but will with the temptation also make a way to escape, that ye may be able to bear it.

1 Corinthians 10:13 KJV

UNDERSTAND:

Paul warns the Corinthians that the lure of idolatry and sexual immorality must be dealt with lest those who fall prey suffer the consequences. He also includes today's verse as an encouragement that we needn't fall for the lure. In what ways are you vulnerable to temptation?

....

....

Why are those who stand alone most likely to fall into temptation?

....

....

....

How can you better protect your own eyes—and your children's eyes—from the temptations of the world?

....

....

....

APPLY:

Temptation is common to all men. Even Jesus faced temptation. If we are to stand firm against temptation like Jesus, we'll need to live like Jesus did. That means staying close to the Father through prayer, being immersed in God's Word, and honoring God with our bodies.

The temptation of sexual immorality is especially prevalent today, when pornography is readily available and society has normalized selfish indulgences of all kinds. But just because everyone does something doesn't make it right. It is better all around to flee temptation when it shows up, and to stay away from situations you know will lead to temptation.

You aren't just doing this for you. By keeping things like pornography out of your home, you're protecting your kids from becoming wired toward those temptations.

And you're not alone in this. Literally every guy is tempted by something. Together, and with God's help, you can escape the dangers of temptation.

PRAY:

Lord, protect my mind from being tempted by things that would hurt our relationship. Keep me close to You so the things of this world won't be so tempting. May I keep my home free from sin, lest I introduce a stumbling block for my children. Amen.

FORGIVE YOUR FATHER

Read Romans 5

KEY VERSE:

But God shows his love for us in that while we were still sinners, Christ died for us.
ROMANS 5:8 ESV

UNDERSTAND:

According to Romans 5:3–5, what are the benefits of suffering?

God didn't let the fact that we were enemies stop Him from rescuing us from sin. Why do we sometimes resist accepting forgiveness now that we are His children?

God made the first move in making our relationship right. How can you make the first move in relationships that need help in your life?

APPLY:

Aside from our Father in heaven, no father is perfect. You aren't perfect (sorry you had to find out this way). Your dad wasn't either. In fact, you can probably think of some significant ways that your dad wasn't perfect. You might even carry some past hurts around with you due to the ways you and your dad clashed.

Whether or not your dad is still around, you can take the first step toward reconciliation. If God could forgive us while we were still actively opposed to Him, you can forgive your dad for the ways he hurt you in the past. Forgiveness isn't something that requires reconciliation, but you can't get to reconciliation without it.

As you raise your kids, you'll undoubtedly mess things up, but showing them that they don't have to carry around their hurts is a godly parenting move that will improve your relationship for years to come.

PRAY:

Lord, thanks for forgiving me before I deserved it. Help me forgive like You. Whether my dad did the best for me or not, I leave him in Your hands and thank You for the path that has led me to You. May I be a godly example for my kids of someone who depends on Your grace. Amen.

TAKE ANOTHER DAD UNDER YOUR WING

Read 1 Peter 5:1–11

KEY VERSES:

Be shepherds of God's flock that is under your care, watching over them—not because you must, but because you are willing, as God wants you to be; not pursuing dishonest gain, but eager to serve; not lording it over those entrusted to you, but being examples to the flock.

1 Peter 5:2–3 NIV

UNDERSTAND:

According to today's passage, what is the reward for watching out for those who have less experience than you?

....

....

First Peter 5:8 says that the devil is on the prowl. Why is it easier to resist him and stand firm when you know that other Christians are experiencing the same kind of devilish attention?

....

....

....

What does Peter pray for the recipients of his letter in verse 10? How can you pray this for yourself?

....

....

....

APPLY:

Unless you're reading this book on the way home from the hospital with your first child strapped into the car seat behind you, you've got some experience in parenting. If you are reading this on the way home from the hospital, stop reading and pay attention to the road.

You may not know everything there is about being a dad, but you know something. You may not consider yourself to be a shepherd of God's flock, but you can still be a leader who helps out where there are needs. And dads need other dads!

As Proverbs 27:17 (NIV) says, "As iron sharpens iron, so one person sharpens another."

So find a dad with younger kids and find out how you can help him. Answer any questions he has. Ask questions yourself. In working together, you can sharpen each other to be the most useful tools in your church's parenting toolbox.

PRAY:

Lord, connect me with other dads who have questions I can answer. Connect me with answers to the questions I don't know. Always help me rely on the wisdom in Your Word more than whatever I think is right. Amen.

ACCEPT REBUKE WELL

Read 2 Samuel 12:1–15

KEY VERSE:

David said to Nathan, "I have sinned against the Lord." And Nathan said to David, "The Lord also has put away your sin; you shall not die."
2 Samuel 12:13 ESV

UNDERSTAND:

In the aftermath of David's plot to take Bathsheba for himself and murder her husband, the Lord sent Nathan, a prophet, to rebuke David. Why do you think Nathan's method of telling the story about a rich man who steals a poor man's lamb was so effective?

What defense does David offer to Nathan's rebuke?

How does David accept the consequences for his actions?

APPLY:

Being rebuked is no fun. In David's case, the Lord sent the prophet Nathan to call him out for the murder of one of David's own mighty men and for exercising his position as king to take Bathsheba for himself. Those are serious crimes! If David treated his friends like that, Nathan might have been justifiably nervous about calling David out.

But although David did serious wrong, he was still a man after God's own heart. He listened to Nathan, understood the seriousness of his crimes, and immediately confessed, ready to accept whatever consequences the Lord saw fit to give him.

When you are rebuked for some wrong you've committed, how do you react? Do you double down and insist you've done nothing wrong? Do you seek to shift the blame? Or do you man up, admit your shortcomings, and accept the consequences like a man after God's own heart?

PRAY:

Lord, I want to be a man after Your own heart. Don't let me wait until rebuke comes to admit my need for grace and forgiveness. But when I am called out, help me accept the rebuke well. Keep my heart soft and teachable so my kids can see how, even when I'm in the wrong, I can live with honor. Amen.

STAND UP FOR THE OPPRESSED

Read Isaiah 1:1–20

KEY VERSES:

Wash yourselves; make yourselves clean; remove the evil of your deeds from before my eyes; cease to do evil, learn to do good; seek justice, correct oppression; bring justice to the fatherless, plead the widow's cause.

Isaiah 1:16–17 ESV

UNDERSTAND:

Isaiah calls the heavens and earth as a witness against God's chosen people in a kind of trial judgment. What are the people accused of?

How does God feel about sacrifices and celebrations that are given in word only instead of as a result of an authentic expression of need and love?

What does God promise in verses 18–20 if His people return to Him?

APPLY:

If you want to see what a society values, watch how it treats those who cannot contribute. In ancient Israel, there was no one more helpless in society than widows and orphans. Because property passed from male to nearest-living male relative, women were exceptionally vulnerable when not provided for by a father or husband.

If God's people were living with hearts full of His values, their society would have readily stepped up to care for widows and orphans, providing them with the housing and protection they lacked. But it is easy to ignore the cries of those whom society has made voiceless through lack of power.

Today's society may be arranged differently in relation to property ownership, but there are still oppressed people. How are you seeking justice for those who wouldn't naturally get it? How would you hope society would care for your family if you weren't there to protect them?

....

....

....

....

....

....

....

....

....

PRAY:

Lord, it is too easy to ignore the needs of the voiceless. Open my ears to their cries. Open my eyes to their needs. Soften my heart and strengthen my resolve to seek out practical ways to bring justice to those who are often denied it. Amen.

BE GENEROUS

Read 2 Corinthians 8:1–15, 9:6–15

KEY VERSES:

Each of you should give what you have decided in your heart to give, not reluctantly or under compulsion, for God loves a cheerful giver. And God is able to bless you abundantly, so that in all things at all times, having all that you need, you will abound in every good work.

2 Corinthians 9:7–8 NIV

UNDERSTAND:

Today's passage opens with the example of generosity shown by the Macedonian church to Paul. What do you think it means that they "gave themselves first of all to the Lord, and then by the will of God also to us" (2 Corinthians 8:5 NIV)?

....

....

....

....

....

According to 2 Corinthians 9:10–11, what is the purpose of God's generosity to us?

....

....

....

....

....

APPLY:

The world would like you to live with a scarcity mindset. If you believe that resources are scarce, you'll pay more than necessary, you'll buy more than you need, and you do it faster than anyone else. Think about times when basic commodities like toilet paper, bread, and disinfecting wipes were hard to find, and you'll get the idea.

The problem with the scarcity mindset—aside from its encouragement toward unhealthy buying habits—is that it just isn't true! God has wired the world to be generous. Every plant God made carries the ability to make seeds and grow more plants.

Through our life in the Holy Spirit, we are wired to be generous as well. When we give of our resources with a cheerful heart, God will multiply our resources in order to achieve His purposes. We get to partner with God's generosity, not so we can hoard basic resources but so others will see God's generosity by giving resources away.

PRAY:

Father, You've been generous in millions of ways toward me. May I live with open hands to the needs around me. Help my children see that I love You more than the things You've blessed me with. May I teach them to be generous by word and deed. Amen.

DON'T COMPLAIN

Read Philippians 2:1–18

KEY VERSES:

Do all things without grumbling or disputing, that you may be blameless and innocent, children of God without blemish in the midst of a crooked and twisted generation, among whom you shine as lights in the world.

PHILIPPIANS 2:14–15 ESV

UNDERSTAND:

Philippians 2 shares how Jesus humbled Himself by taking human form and submitting to death on a cross. How can you have Christ's mindset in this way?

....

....

....

What is the relationship between humility and complaining?

....

....

....

....

How might you better shine your light so others can see God's love?

....

....

....

....

APPLY:

You know when you ask your kids to do something they don't want to do? They'll do it, eventually, after you've hounded them a bit, but they do it with that look on their face that says, "I'm only doing this because I have to, but I'd rather be doing anything else."

Hopefully, this scenario doesn't happen every time you give your kids a job, but it probably sounds familiar. How much better would it be if they just did the thing without dragging their feet or shooting dirty looks? It would be done in no time, and they could get back to whatever it is they want to do.

But it isn't just kids who do this, right?

God has given us all jobs to do, and not all of them will be fun. When we grumble and drag our feet, we're only hurting ourselves and our witness to the world.

....

....

....

....

....

....

....

....

....

PRAY:

Father, forgive me for the times when my bad attitude hinders Your message of love. Help me do Your will with a great attitude, even when it doesn't fit into my plans. May I combat grumbling with praise and complaining with thankfulness. Amen.

BE WILLING TO ADAPT

Read Acts 9:1–22

KEY VERSE:

And all who heard him were amazed and said, "Is not this the man who made havoc in Jerusalem of those who called upon this name? And has he not come here for this purpose, to bring them bound before the chief priests?"

Acts 9:21 ESV

UNDERSTAND:

Saul (aka Paul) was an intense follower of the Hebrew law, going so far as to persecute those he saw as preaching heresy. Ananias had heard about Saul's reputation and mission and questioned the wisdom of Jesus in healing Saul's blindness. How did Jesus answer Ananias' fears?

....

....

....

....

....

How have you questioned God's wisdom when He asked you to do something you were afraid to do?

....

....

....

....

....

APPLY:

Saul had a reputation for piety and intensity. In Philippians 3:5–6 (ESV), he says he was "circumcised on the eighth day, of the people of Israel, of the tribe of Benjamin, a Hebrew of Hebrews; as to the law, a Pharisee; as to zeal, a persecutor of the church; as to righteousness under the law, blameless."

As faithful Jewish followers go, Saul was one of the best. But being the best didn't stop him from being wrong.

When Saul was struck down by the vision of Jesus on his way to flush the Christians out of Damascus, he realized that everything he was working toward was wrong. He spent three days fasting and praying, blinded by Christ's light, but was finally able to see things clearly. Saul adapted to new truths and lived for Christ as intensely as he had previously lived for the law.

When presented with new information, are you quick to adapt or are you stuck in your opinions and ways?

PRAY:

Lord, blind me to anything that isn't from You. Open my eyes to new truths You want me to live in. As I learn and grow in my faith and in my fatherhood, help me adapt smoothly so I can better represent You to my kids and community. Amen.

SEE A NEED, FILL A NEED

Read Matthew 25:31–46

KEY VERSES:

"For I was hungry and you gave me something to eat, I was thirsty and you gave me something to drink, I was a stranger and you invited me in, I needed clothes and you clothed me, I was sick and you looked after me, I was in prison and you came to visit me."

MATTHEW 25:35–36 NIV

UNDERSTAND:

Today's passage says that "all the nations" (verse 32) will be gathered before Jesus on His throne. How does this glimpse of the future relate to the Great Commission (see Matthew 28:19–20)?

....

....

....

....

The sheep and the goats act differently toward the needs around them, but it isn't their actions that separate the two groups; it is their relationship with the Father. How do the sheep's identity as inheritors of God's kingdom inspire them to act?

....

....

....

....

....

APPLY:

Robots, an animated kids' movie from 2005, centers around Rodney Copperbottom, a young inventor who seeks his fortune in the big city. Along the way, Rodney joins a ragtag group of robotic rejects to uncover the disappearance of the city's former inventing genius, Bigweld. While Rodney goes about his mission, he fixes broken robots and inspires hope among the downtrodden, echoing the catchphrase of his hero, Bigweld: "See a need, fill a need."

Rodney's story shares a biblical concept in a fun way. As children of God, we are called to mimic our Maker, caring for others as God would until we get to the final judgment. We are aided by the indwelling of the Holy Spirit, who helps us see the world through spiritual eyes so we can notice the needs of others. We may not even realize the ways we are serving Christ by caring for His people, but we are.

Why not have a family movie night and discuss what it means to "see a need, fill a need" with your kids this weekend?

PRAY:

Lord, my actions toward others reflect my relationship with You. Help me see the needs of others and fill them according to Your love. Amen.

BE PRESENT

Read Luke 10:38–42, John 12:1–8

KEY VERSES:

But the Lord answered her, "Martha, Martha,
you are anxious and troubled about many things,
but one thing is necessary. Mary has chosen the good
portion, which will not be taken away from her."
Luke 10:41–42 ESV

UNDERSTAND:

Mary and Martha have very different priorities. Whom do you identify with more strongly?

....

....

....

How do the two different scenes of Mary show examples of what Jesus finds important?

....

....

....

When Judas suggested that Mary could have used her money more wisely, why was his suggestion frowned upon?

....

....

....

....

APPLY:

People with to-do lists get things done. And when you're in task mode, there's nothing more satisfying than crossing things off your to-do list. Habitual list makers even begin their lists with "Make a list" just so they can cross it off. But what if while we're making lists and crossing things off, we're missing out on what is truly important?

Although the Bible doesn't specifically say so, you can bet that Martha was a list maker. Mary, her sister, was content to live in the moment. Mary had a knack for seeing what was needed in the moment instead of filling her moments with various needs.

As a dad, how do you do at seeing the needs of your family? Do you get hung up on lists, or are you able to put them down so you can play catch, work on a family puzzle, or read a book together? Don't miss out on what's important because you're too busy to see it.

PRAY:

Father, give me wisdom to know what is most important to You each moment of the day. Help me fulfill my responsibilities while not missing out on helping my kids feel seen and loved. Amen.

FIGHT MATERIALISM

Read 1 Timothy 6

KEY VERSE:

For the love of money is a root of all kinds of evil. Some people, eager for money, have wandered from the faith and pierced themselves with many griefs.

1 Timothy 6:10 NIV

UNDERSTAND:

After reading today's passage, how would you define contentment?

Paul writes a great pep talk to Timothy in verses 11–12. How can you better pursue what Paul recommends?

How does Paul want Timothy to approach the rich in verses 17–19? Would you consider yourself to be rich in good deeds?

APPLY:

We all want to have enough, but wouldn't it be better to have *more* than enough? Well, it depends.

Some people want to be rich so they can buy the latest gadgets, go out to eat all the time, and have a big enough house for all the stuff they want to buy. But 1 Timothy 6:9 (NIV) says, "Those who want to get rich fall into temptation and a trap and into many foolish and harmful desires that plunge people into ruin and destruction."

That doesn't mean rich people are evil or that the desire to have more than you need is bad. You just need to realize that earthly riches should be used to create godly riches (see verses 18–19).

When your kids start asking for more toys, bigger playrooms, and better gadgets, remind them—by word and deed—that contentment is better, and riches are simply fuel for generosity.

PRAY:

Father, may I model the godliness with contentment that leads to great gain, and recognize the gains You've already provided. May my children see me strive not for more earthly goods but for heavenly treasures. Amen.

LIVE IN THE LIGHT

Read John 3:1–21

KEY VERSES:

For God did not send his Son into the world to condemn the world, but in order that the world might be saved through him. Whoever believes in him is not condemned, but whoever does not believe is condemned already, because he has not believed in the name of the only Son of God.

JOHN 3:17–18 ESV

UNDERSTAND:

John 3:16 is one of the most famous verses of the Bible. To a ruler of the Jews like Nicodemus, it must have been shocking. The Jews were looking for the Messiah to rescue Israel from oppression, but Jesus offers eternal life to anyone who believes in Him. How do you think Nicodemus felt about the difference between his hopes and Jesus' offer?

....

....

....

....

In verses 19–21, Jesus discusses light and darkness. Are you living so your deeds would be good to see in the light?

....

....

....

....

APPLY:

Have you ever tried to cook tacos in the dark? No. Why would you? You'd want to see what's happening in the pan, to make sure that the meat has been cooked thoroughly, and to make sure that the seasonings are measured properly. You need light to do a job well.

Doing something in darkness means you don't want other people to see you. It's silly to think of cooking tacos in the dark because who cares if you're making tacos? But this isn't really about tacos, is it?

The lights are always on with God because God is light. If you think doing things in darkness will fool anyone, you're only fooling yourself. The people you are hiding things from don't have the power to condemn you; only the God who already sees what you are up to does.

Next time you catch your kids doing something they were trying to hide, remember that God is light. Help them find forgiveness and live in the light from now on.

PRAY:

Lord of light, my deeds are all made clear to You. I am not condemned, because I have faith in Your sacrifice. May I live without fear or the need to hide anything. May my kids see my lifestyle and live in Your light as well. Amen.

KEEP YOUR PRIORITIES STRAIGHT

Read Deuteronomy 6

KEY VERSE:

And thou shalt love the Lord thy God with all thine heart, and with all thy soul, and with all thy might.

Deuteronomy 6:5 KJV

UNDERSTAND:

Why is it important to communicate God's truth with your children?

How will you answer your kids when they ask why it is important to learn about God's truth?

How can you keep your priorities straight with God at the top of the list?

APPLY:

When kids come along, your life turns upside down. If you are married, your household grows by at least 50 percent, and the newest resident's needs take up about 90 percent of any previous free time. It's easy to think your kids are now the most important thing in your life, based on nothing more than the amount of time they require.

The problem with this approach to parenting is that when the kids move out, a lot of married folk realize they no longer know their partners. Sadly, divorce is common among empty nesters who were only staying together for the kids.

As a dad, it's important to keep *all* your priorities straight, and while marriage shouldn't occupy the top slot, neither should your kids. God always needs to come first! Marriage second. Kids a distant third.

When you live according to these priorities, every one of these relationships will flourish, just as God intended.

PRAY:

Father, be my top priority. Help me know that my kids are not more important than You, that my wife is not more important than You, that nothing is more important than You. Help me love my wife accordingly so we don't get to the empty-nest stage and realize we don't know each other. Amen.

DON'T NEGLECT SELF-CARE

Read Mark 1:9–45

KEY VERSE:

And rising very early in the morning, while it was still dark, he departed and went out to a desolate place, and there he prayed.

MARK 1:35 ESV

UNDERSTAND:

Today's passage is a fire-hose introduction to Jesus' ministry. What stands out to you as you read how Jesus came onto the scene?

Why is it surprising that Jesus chose fishermen to follow Him? If Jesus called you to be His disciple, would you drop everything and follow?

APPLY:

It didn't take long for word to get around about Jesus' ministry. He taught with authority. He healed the sick, cast out demons, and touched those whom society had kicked to the margins. Jesus was a different kind of rabbi!

As God in the flesh, it isn't surprising that He did things differently. What might be surprising is that He took time to recharge. Today's verse tells us that Jesus found time, early in the morning, to pray. He recharged by connecting with God before the many needs of the day began.

I don't know what time it is while you read this. I don't know what your schedule looks like. What I do know is that you are probably busy. You probably need to recharge before the needs of the day wear you down.

Remember, even Jesus took time to care for His mental and spiritual health, and He was Jesus!

PRAY:

Jesus, You took time away from Your ministry to make sure You could do Your ministry. Don't let me run dry because I'm trying to tackle things without You. I need Your strength in my weakness. Fill me today. Amen.

DO GOOD AND DON'T GROW WEARY

Read Galatians 6

KEY VERSE:

Therefore, as we have opportunity, let us do good to all people, especially to those who belong to the family of believers.

GALATIANS 6:10 NIV

UNDERSTAND:

Today's passage tells believers to carry each other's burdens (v. 2) and to carry their own load (verse 5). How is this double-carrying mentality possible (hint: see verse 18)?

....

....

....

....

....

We will reap what we sow, but what more than sowing is implied in verses 9–10?

....

....

....

....

....

....

APPLY:

The church isn't a building, though that's an easy mistake to make. The church is meant to be a plural noun, referring to the multitude of believers. Today's verse refers to it as a family.

That fits.

Families are messy and require almost constant mediation, grace, and help from God to stay close. You can tell the difference between family members who care how their actions affect others and those who don't—either because they are too young and unaware or because they are too far into their own desires to be easily pulled out.

But the Bible doesn't want us to leave family members headed toward destruction. We shouldn't want that either!

So how can we bring them back toward the big family hug that is the church? We show them that we value them. We restore them gently. We carry both our load and their load with the grace of God carrying us. Your kids will need this, sure, but so will everyone at some point. Don't get weary. The harvest is coming.

....

....

....

....

....

....

....

....

PRAY:

Father, as You have restored me with Your love, help me restore others. May I sow good seed to please the Spirit instead of myself. Help me not grow weary, because I'll be filled with Your strength. Amen.

DON'T IMMEDIATELY REACT

Read Proverbs 14

KEY VERSE:

Whoever is slow to anger has great understanding,
but he who has a hasty temper exalts folly.
PROVERBS 14:29 ESV

UNDERSTAND:

The proverbs explain concepts by contrasting two ideas. When read together, we get a mental image of living wisely. While the proverbs can be applied individually, sometimes they paint a fuller picture when read together. How is that the case with verses 20–21?

Which proverbs about the importance of wisdom make you want to live more wisely?

APPLY:

Imagine: You come home to find that your child has broken something you cherished. What happens next?

Maybe you count to ten. Ideally, you should count to ninety. Why? It takes ninety seconds for the chemicals released by the brain to flow through your system when you are faced with a stressful stimulus—something that triggers your "fight, flight, or freeze" response. And as you view the destruction of that cherished thing, you're probably feeling those chemicals course through you.

Your brain has prepped you for a response that has nothing to do with calm words or seeking understanding, but reacting immediately with anger is not the right response. When you notice your body being flooded by chemicals, start counting. After the ninety-second mark, think about what you value more: that broken thing or your child. Now take a deep breath and ask what happened.

....

....

....

....

....

....

....

....

....

PRAY:

Lord, You've always been patient with me,
no matter how badly I've broken things.
Give me perspective as I am faced with anger,
stress, and issues of justice. Keep me far from
folly and close to understanding. Amen.

HAVE A PARENTAL PLAYDATE

Read Hebrews 10:19–39

KEY VERSES:

And let us consider how to stir up one another to love and good works, not neglecting to meet together, as is the habit of some, but encouraging one another, and all the more as you see the Day drawing near.

Hebrews 10:24–25 ESV

UNDERSTAND:

According to verses 19–23, what does faith allow us to do?

....

....

....

In verse 26 (ESV), the author of Hebrews says, "If we go on sinning deliberately after receiving the knowledge of the truth, there no longer remains a sacrifice for sins," but the author isn't suggesting that believers lose their salvation. What is he talking about?

....

....

....

What does true enlightenment look like according to verses 32–39?

....

....

....

....

APPLY:

There's that old saying that it takes a village to raise a child, and that's true. No parent can successfully manage the rigors of parenthood without help—both help from God and from other responsible adults He's placed in your life.

And as important as it is to lean on people when you need advice on potty training or how to build a campfire the right way or whatever, it's even more important to support each other in spiritual matters. Today's verses encourage people of faith to stir each other up to good works in light of the approaching end days.

By meeting together and living in light of Jesus' sacrifice as a community, we'll make sure we aren't fooling ourselves concerning the state of our soul, and we'll make it possible to endure the struggles that result from faithful living.

Where can you find this spiritual support group? Start at church, spread to the community, and talk to the parents of your kids' friends. It doesn't matter how it starts as long as you know where it is heading.

PRAY:

Lord, surround me with those who will encourage me to follow You through good times and affliction. Help me support them with good works and words of encouragement. Amen.

REMEMBER THAT BROKENNESS IS TEMPORARY

Read Revelation 21

KEY VERSES:

And I heard a loud voice from the throne saying, "Behold, the dwelling place of God is with man. He will dwell with them, and they will be his people, and God himself will be with them as their God. He will wipe away every tear from their eyes, and death shall be no more, neither shall there be mourning, nor crying, nor pain anymore, for the former things have passed away."

REVELATION 21:3–4 ESV

UNDERSTAND:

How does the promise from today's verse echo the promises God gave to the nation of Israel?

....

....

Who is seated on the throne in verse 5? How can you tell?

....

....

....

Why is there no temple in the city of God?

....

....

....

APPLY:

We live in a broken world. Our cnvironment is broken. Our governments are broken. Our workplaces are broken. We are broken. And even the things that aren't broken yet are in the process of breaking down. It might be depressing if brokenness was the ultimate end of our existence.

But it's not.

This brokenness is temporary. There's a time coming—an eternity—when God will dwell with His people in a city that has no need of sun or moon, because the glory of God gives it light!

The next time your kiddo brings you a broken toy or breaks a bone or reveals some brokenness inherent in society, remember that this is temporary. And temporary things are endurable because the best is yet to come!

PRAY:

Father, give me strength to endure the brokenness. Use the brokenness within me for Your everlasting light to shine through the cracks. Help me raise my kids so they know how to become whole in You. Thank You for loving me. I can't wait to be with You forever! Amen.

TURN OFF THE SCREEN

Read Proverbs 24

KEY VERSES:

I passed by the field of a sluggard, by the vineyard of a man lacking sense, and behold, it was all overgrown with thorns; the ground was covered with nettles, and its stone wall was broken down.

PROVERBS 24:30–31 ESV

UNDERSTAND:

According to today's reading, how is your house built?

....

....

....

Verse 16 says that the righteous falls seven times and rises again. Why are the righteous able to get back up when the wicked stumble and stay down?

....

....

....

....

Why is it important to do things in the right order, according to verse 27?

....

....

....

....

APPLY:

Have you ever seen old-timey photos of life before television? People sat around and stared at the radio. There's something in our brains that craves new information, stopping us in our tracks and turning our faces toward whatever promises that informative edge to help us survive.

Screens are everywhere today! In the living room, at work, at restaurants, in our pockets! If you aren't intentional with limiting your screen time, it's possible to spend the majority of every day staring at that glowing rectangle, mesmerized. And you are (supposed to be) a responsible adult! Consider your kids and how their little brains are being wired to stare at screens.

Are there good things to watch during screen time? Sure. But how can you work God's garden toward the harvest if you never look away from your phone? The vineyard is already full of thorns. It's time to look up and start working toward the harvest.

....

....

....

....

....

....

....

....

PRAY:

Lord, help me limit the time I spend in front of a screen. Help me set the right example for my kids so they can grow up with healthy attention spans, able to work in different ways to honor You. Grow in me a desire to work in Your spiritual fields. Amen.

SHARE THE PARENTING RESPONSIBILITIES EQUITABLY

Read 1 Timothy 5:1–22

KEY VERSE:

Anyone who does not provide for their relatives, and especially for their own household, has denied the faith and is worse than an unbeliever.

1 Timothy 5:8 NIV

UNDERSTAND:

Paul's letter to Timothy advises the young pastor on how to care for different groups within the church, treating each group as family. How do you treat the different groups mentioned in this passage?

....

....

....

Why is the church's responsibility different between widows with support systems and those without?

....

....

....

What warnings does Paul give to Timothy concerning potential leaders within the church?

....

....

....

APPLY:

In His earthly ministry, Christ specifically helped widows, orphans, and other marginalized groups. Caring for those who had no one else was evidence that God's love is for everyone, not just for the privileged within society. As the body of Christ, the church is dedicated to carrying out Christ's mission toward the marginalized.

What does that have to do with you, if you aren't a widower and your kids aren't orphans? For dads who prioritize their own interests—their job, their hobbies, their time with other guys—there isn't much difference between their family and those families of widows and orphans.

And since today's verse specifically calls out Christians who refuse to care for their own distant family members in need, why not start closer to home? When your kids are sick, do you take time off to care for them? Do you divide and conquer household tasks with your spouse?

It's time for dads to step up and get involved on a whole new level!

PRAY:

Lord, open my eyes to the ways I've neglected my responsibilities at home. Don't let my spouse and kids be widows and orphans by another name just because I am busy with my own interests. Amen.

COLOR WITH ALL THE CRAYONS

Read Revelation 7

KEY VERSES:

After this I looked, and there before me was a great multitude that no one could count, from every nation, tribe, people and language, standing before the throne and before the Lamb. They were wearing white robes and were holding palm branches in their hands. And they cried out in a loud voice: "Salvation belongs to our God, who sits on the throne, and to the Lamb."

Revelation 7:9–10 NIV

UNDERSTAND:

Revelation is a difficult book to interpret, but we can use it to learn more about the God we serve even if we don't understand specifically what is taking place during the end times. What does this passage tell us about God?

....

....

Why is it significant that a great multitude from every nation stands before God's throne?

....

....

How does verse 17 describe Jesus today, not just in the future?

....

....

....

APPLY:

If you've ever gone to a restaurant that gives kids a small pack of crayons to color on the children's menu while you wait for your meal, you'll understand the frustrating limitations caused by a lack of diversity. Maybe you wouldn't have thought of it like that, but when you compare the three or four crayons that come in those restaurant packs to the box of sixty-four crayons you might have at home, you get it.

God's plan has always been for a diverse body of believers—representatives from every nation, tribe, people, and language—to spend time with Him and to enjoy His loving care for eternity.

People who attempt to limit who has access to God's love by denying the need for diversity are like people who prefer a four-pack of crayons to the larger pack. Crazy!

The next time you color with your kids—and every kid loves coloring no matter how old they are—tell them that God's picture of heaven includes everyone.

PRAY:

Father, may I treat all people with respect and love, valuing them as people made in Your image. Help me appreciate our differences and similarities and welcome them to stand beside me at the foot of Your throne, praising You in our unique ways. May my kids see my example and embrace diversity too. Amen.

BE PATIENT

Read James 5

KEY VERSES:

Be patient, therefore, brothers, until the coming of the Lord. See how the farmer waits for the precious fruit of the earth, being patient about it, until it receives the early and the late rains. You also, be patient. Establish your hearts, for the coming of the Lord is at hand.

JAMES 5:7–8 ESV

UNDERSTAND:

While some men will do just about anything to get rich, what does today's passage say about riches?

....

....

....

James looks to the Old Testament prophets as an example of patience in action. What were the prophets waiting for?

....

....

....

How does faith play into the concept of patience?

....

....

....

APPLY:

Kids go through stages. There's the diaper phase (where you learn that being covered in feces is just part of parental life), the crawling phase (where you learn that things are replaceable now that your child can reach and destroy more), and the walking phase (where you learn to smile in spite of the fact that your child just fell down and whacked their head, but they are looking at you to see how they are supposed to react). Each phase is temporary and sometimes only appreciated in hindsight.

You might be looking forward to the current phase ending because you're excited about the next one. That's where patience comes in. Patience is actively waiting for something better while currently appreciating what God's given you.

When you are patient as a dad, you can better appreciate the stage your kids are in. It doesn't lessen what is coming, but it establishes your heart in God's perfect timing.

PRAY:

Lord, when I wish time was moving faster, help me be patient. When my kids are driving me nuts with the phase they are in, help me be patient. When my life feels out of control, help me be patient. You are always patient with me. Amen.

REMEMBER WHO MATTERS MOST

Read Genesis 22:1–19

KEY VERSE:

And he said, Take now thy son, thine only son Isaac, whom thou lovest, and get thee into the land of Moriah; and offer him there for a burnt offering upon one of the mountains which I will tell thee of.

Genesis 22:2 KJV

UNDERSTAND:

When Abraham understood what God required of him, how long did he wait to accomplish it?

....

....

How did God's provision of a ram foreshadow the substitutionary sacrifice of Jesus on the cross?

....

....

....

God had already promised Abraham many descendants through Isaac. Now He was asking Abraham to sacrifice him. What do you think Abraham was thinking?

....

....

....

....

APPLY:

God promised Abraham that his offspring would be as numerous as the stars in the sky. Abraham waited and waited—albeit not always patiently—and at age one hundred, he fathered Isaac. Isaac was a miracle baby who was going to help fulfill God's promise to Abraham.

Then God told Abraham to head to the land of Moriah and offer Isaac as a burnt sacrifice. Plot twist! Abraham waited decades for the fulfillment of God's promise, but He trusted God and immediately followed His directions.

You may not be one hundred years old, but the fact that you are a father is miraculous. God might not have promised you billions of offspring, but you love your kids to the stars and back, right?

Loving your kids is important, but do you love God more? Things worked out for Abraham and Isaac because Abraham knew that God wouldn't fail to come through for him.

PRAY:

Father God, You are more important than my desires, my blessings, my marriage, and my children. Help me remember to keep my priorities straight. When You ask me to sacrifice the things I think are important, help me remember what is most important. Amen.

ASK FOR WHAT YOU NEED; NEED THE RIGHT THINGS

Read James 4

KEY VERSE:

You desire but do not have, so you kill. You covet but you cannot get what you want, so you quarrel and fight. You do not have because you do not ask God.

James 4:2 NIV

UNDERSTAND:

Today's passage draws a stark contrast between peaceful godliness and quarrelsome selfishness. When you read through each verse, ask God to show you the ways your motivations have led you to ask for the wrong things.

Do you ever ask for the right things but at the wrong time?

How have you been guilty of knowing the right thing to do and failing to do it?

APPLY:

Some kids are naturally gifted in asking for things. There are no limits to their requests. They ask for cookies, toys, video games, pets, candy, and more, all before breakfast. Then if they don't immediately get what they ask for, they get angry, sullen, or violent. Some kids grow up to become adults who do the same thing.

There is an art to requesting things, the first step of which is requesting the right things. When our requests are motivated by selfish desires—bigger houses, faster cars, tastier food, more money than your neighbors have—they reveal where our heart is. Why would God honor requests that take us further from Him?

The answer isn't to stop requesting things from God but to request the right things at the right times. Just like you want to give your children what is best for them, God wants to bless you!

....

....

....

....

....

....

....

....

....

PRAY:

Father, search my heart and show me what is motivating my requests. Bless me in the ways that will honor You most. May I have enough to share and the desire to match. Help me give my children good things and reinforce their desires to ask for the right things at the right times. Amen.

RIGHT YOUR WRONGS

Read Leviticus 5

KEY VERSE:

"He shall also make restitution for what he has done amiss in the holy thing and shall add a fifth to it and give it to the priest. And the priest shall make atonement for him with the ram of the guilt offering, and he shall be forgiven."
LEVITICUS 5:16 ESV

UNDERSTAND:

Leviticus offers a glimpse into Old Testament life under the law. The theme in today's passage is that actions—whether intentional or unintentional—have consequences. What examples stand out to you?

....

....

....

How does the law make provision for those who cannot afford certain sacrifices?

....

....

....

How does the principle of restitution still apply, even though we live under grace instead of under the law?

....

....

....

APPLY:

Are you familiar with the concept of "You break it, you buy it"? The saying is a snappy reminder to be careful with property that doesn't belong to you. If you've ever taken your kids into a store where there are breakable things everywhere, you might have uttered it yourself.

In the Old Testament, people were responsible for making restitution for laws they broke. It wasn't enough to simply pay the sin offering; they were to add a fifth of the amount on top of that for the priests. This would help cover the priests' livelihood as well as serve as a costly reminder to avoid that sin in the future.

When Jesus died for our sins, He canceled the debts we would have to pay because He was the perfect sacrifice, but that doesn't mean we can break things and sin willy-nilly. If we break something, we are still best off buying it. Why? Because our actions reflect on the one who purchased our debts on the cross.

....

....

....

....

....

....

....

....

....

PRAY:

Father, may I always make right the ways I've wronged others. I cannot repay You for Your grace, but I can show the world what it looks like to be Your child. Help my own kids see me take responsibility for my actions so they understand why restitution is still necessary today. Amen.

REMEMBER THE GOLDEN RULE

Read Luke 6:27–45

KEY VERSE:

Do to others as you would have them do to you.
Luke 6:31 NIV

UNDERSTAND:

Hopefully, you don't consider your children to be your enemies, but how does Luke 6:27–31 fit well with parenting?

How can you avoid hypocrisy in your parenting?

What kind of fruit does your tree grow? Is it recognizable to everyone?

APPLY:

Parenting can be a thankless job. You do your best for your kids. You try to get them to eat good things. You set boundaries so they'll be safe. What do you get in return?

Bad attitudes. Muttered curses or angry yells. Sullen or dirty looks.

It'd be easy to answer the attitudes and behaviors in kind, to yell back when being yelled at, but that's the world's way of handling frustration. We're called to a higher way of living. When Christ was taken to the cross to pay a debt He didn't owe, He didn't fight back. He took the punishment He didn't deserve because He knew what was waiting on the other side of the cross.

Today, you've got the Holy Spirit living inside you, enabling you to choose the higher way of living. When you've got thankless kids, you do right by them anyway. You love them even when they don't seem to be loving you in return. Because you are Dad. . .and because you are God's child.

PRAY:

Lord, give me patience when I feel like retaliating. Help me choose the higher way, even when it feels impossible. You took abuse You didn't deserve and gave me the Holy Spirit so I can follow in Your footsteps. Thank You. Amen.

PRAY, EVEN WHEN YOU CAN'T

Read Romans 8:1–30

KEY VERSE:

Likewise the Spirit helps us in our weakness. For we do not know what to pray for as we ought, but the Spirit himself intercedes for us with groanings too deep for words.

Romans 8:26 ESV

UNDERSTAND:

How might you explain life in the Spirit as opposed to life in the flesh—as described in verses 1–11—to your kids?

....

....

....

What does it mean to be a child of God?

....

....

....

....

All of creation is groaning for the completion of God's renewal. In what ways is this most visible to you?

....

....

....

....

APPLY:

Prayer is awesome. We pray when we praise God for His goodness, His power, and His righteousness. We pray to express our reliance on God's provision. We pray when we request God's help for others. We pray to thank God for the blessings He gives us—even if they feel like curses at the time. But there are times when we don't know how to pray, when we have needs that our minds can't articulate.

As a dad, you know the times when words fail you, when you are so flabbergasted by a situation that the language part of your brain is completely bypassed. This too can be prayer.

All prayer starts with the Holy Spirit inside of us speaking to our Father in heaven by way of Jesus' atoning grace. Prayer is God involving us as He talks to Himself on our behalf. How awesome is that!

....

....

....

....

....

....

....

....

....

....

PRAY:

Holy Spirit, thank You for praying on my behalf when I don't have the words. Jesus, thank You for making it possible for me to approach God's throne with my needs. Father, thank You for loving me through everything. Amen.

WELCOME THE PRODIGAL

Read Luke 15:8–32

KEY VERSE:

And he arose, and came to his father. But when he was yet a great way off, his father saw him, and had compassion, and ran, and fell on his neck, and kissed him.

LUKE 15:20 KJV

UNDERSTAND:

The younger son from Jesus' parable is unpardonably rude to his father, basically wishing him dead so he could get his inheritance. How have you been rude to your earthly father? How about your heavenly Father?

....

....

....

What are the similarities between the two parables in today's reading?

....

....

....

....

How do you think Jesus' original audience heard the parables?

....

....

....

....

APPLY:

The younger son was a schemer. He wanted the best things for himself and basically suggested that his dad would be better off dead so he could get an early inheritance. The father could have rightfully disowned his son right then—which is what everyone in the community would have expected—but he gave him his request instead.

Even when the prodigal son returned, he had schemes to be hired on as one of his father's craftsmen, an honorable position with a decent paycheck that was respected in the community. But before he could even ask for it, his father tackled him in a loving embrace.

The father didn't let the judgments of the community stop him from loving his child. He didn't let his child fulfill his schemes either, restoring his sonship in a move that surprised everyone.

When your child spits in your face and schemes to get their way, how will you love them back to unity?

....

....

....

....

....

....

....

....

....

....

PRAY:

Father, You've never given up on me, even when I scheme against You. Help me love my children with a love that surprises my whole community. Amen.

BE COMPASSIONATE

Read Psalm 103

KEY VERSE:

As a father shows compassion to his children,
so the LORD shows compassion to those who fear him.
PSALM 103:13 ESV

UNDERSTAND:

What are some of the benefits of being God's child?

....

....

....

....

What are some truths about God you can praise Him for?

....

....

....

....

Though your days are like grass, what can you do to leave a lasting impression on your family and in your community?

....

....

....

....

....

APPLY:

The word *compassion* comes from the Latin word *compati,* which means "to suffer with." It's deeper than feeling bad for someone else. It is entering into their suffering alongside them and offering comfort by your presence more than by actively trying to fix things.

That can be hard for men in general and for dads in particular. We don't want to see our kids suffer. We want to fix the problems causing them to suffer. But what if God has a plan for their suffering? What if this is what they need in order to make a change for the better?

When your kids suffer, suffer with them. Express your compassion as God does. Enter in and experience with them so they aren't alone, but pray seriously before attempting to fix what God would rather have broken.

....

....

....

....

....

....

....

....

....

PRAY:

Father, You are always compassionate with me. You have experienced more suffering than I can imagine—on the cross, through rejection, by my disobedience—and You have never stopped loving me. When my child experiences suffering, give me wisdom on how to enter into it with them without needing to fix it. Amen.

CARRY YOUR CHILD THROUGH THEIR WILDERNESS

Read Deuteronomy 1:6–33

KEY VERSES:

"Then I said to you, 'Do not be in dread or afraid of them. The Lord your God who goes before you will himself fight for you, just as he did for you in Egypt before your eyes, and in the wilderness, where you have seen how the Lord your God carried you, as a man carries his son, all the way that you went until you came to this place.'"

Deuteronomy 1:29–31 ESV

UNDERSTAND:

Today's passage is a summary by Moses of how God led His people out of Egypt and toward the Promised Land. What has God led you out of? What is He leading you toward?

Why did the people not immediately take possession of the Promised Land?

APPLY:

Four hundred years of slavery in Egypt took its toll on the Israelites, but God had not forgotten them. He used Moses to lead His people out of Egypt, performing miraculous signs and terrible wonders, parting the sea and destroying their pursuers, providing for their needs and leading them day and night through the wilderness. God led His people with power and love.

But when they were in the wilderness, the people doubted God's intentions. They questioned His love. They made a golden calf to worship, desired to return to their bondage in Egypt, and feared the challenges involved in taking the Promised Land. And still, God held them close like a father with his child.

Your kids know you love them. They've seen the mighty things you've accomplished and know that you'll stand up for them against the problems they face. But that doesn't always mean they'll trust you. They'll experience their own wilderness doubts. And when they do, carry them with love like you always have.

PRAY:

Lord, as You carry me through the tough times in my life, help me carry my children, even when they doubt my love. Amen.

TURN TOWARD YOUR CHILD

Read Malachi 3:1–4:6

KEY VERSE:

And he shall turn the heart of the fathers to the children, and the heart of the children to their fathers, lest I come and smite the earth with a curse.

MALACHI 4:6 KJV

UNDERSTAND:

Israel hoped the Messiah would come with judgment for other nations and love for them. How does Malachi 3 challenge this hope?

....

....

....

If neglecting to tithe is equivalent to robbing from God, what other ways might someone's neglect be as bad as actively wronging God?

....

....

....

....

How is the sun both good for some things and bad for others? How is that like God?

....

....

....

....

APPLY:

In a study with newlyweds, Dr. John Gottman of the Gottman Institute discovered that couples who actively turn toward each other are more than 50 percent more likely to stay married than couples who turn away. What does it mean to turn toward someone? It means to actively respond to some bid for attention from the other person—to stop what you are doing for a minute and engage with them.

As a dad, your kids are always bidding for your attention, often in ways that you can't help but stop what you're doing and give it to them. But the more often you turn away from these bids, the less likely they'll try to engage you.

In today's passage, Malachi imagines a future in which a prophet will come to set things right, and the hearts of fathers and children will be turned toward each other. Jesus has already come and given us the Holy Spirit to help us turn toward God. When we do that, we'll be more likely to turn toward our kids as well.

PRAY:

Jesus, help me turn toward my children when they bid for my attention. Make our relationships strong so they won't turn away when things get difficult. Amen.

TEACH YOUR KIDS ABOUT PERSONAL RESPONSIBILITY

Read Ezekiel 18:1–24

KEY VERSE:

"The one who sins is the one who will die. The child will not share the guilt of the parent, nor will the parent share the guilt of the child. The righteousness of the righteous will be credited to them, and the wickedness of the wicked will be charged against them."

EZEKIEL 18:20 NIV

UNDERSTAND:

Ezekiel 18 opens with a proverb that God seeks to set right. How do you interpret this proverb?

....

....

What is the relationship between a father's righteousness and that of his child?

....

....

....

What hope can be found in verse 22 for fathers who haven't made the best choices?

....

....

....

APPLY:

Physical traits can be passed from father to child. Sometimes athletic abilities are similarly passed down. Wealth—and poverty—can be passed along as well. The socioeconomic situation of parents can influence the prospects of their kids. But sin? Sinfulness is a level playing field where everyone is equally disadvantaged.

Today's passage outlines the lives of three generations of men—a righteous man, his unrighteous son, and a righteous grandchild. God's insistence that each person is responsible for their actions is a lesson we would do well in covering for our kids. You're going to do your best to raise them right, but their relationship with God is their responsibility.

That said, you still have influence with your kids. If they see you enjoying a vibrant spiritual life where God's hope shines in every situation, they will want it for themselves.

PRAY:

Lord, I know I can't make my children come to You, but let them see me living for You and want that for themselves. Amen.

WALK IN THE GOOD WORKS YOU WERE MEANT FOR

Read Ephesians 2

KEY VERSE:

For we are his workmanship, created in Christ Jesus for good works, which God prepared beforehand, that we should walk in them.

EPHESIANS 2:10 ESV

UNDERSTAND:

How did you walk before you came to Christ?

How would you use today's passage to talk to your children about Jesus?

Ephesians 2:18 says that you have access to God the Father. How are you using your direct line to God?

APPLY:

When was the last time you marveled at God's craftsmanship? Look at a sunrise and reflect on the complexity of the world's relationship with our personal star. We experience seasons because of the tilt of the planet. The world is teeming with life because of how God designed every last atom to do a specific job. And when He made humans, He declared us to be the pinnacle of creation, made in His image.

You matter. God made you for a reason. God loves you, and He desires a close relationship with you. If you love God in return, consider the reason you were made.

God has tasked you with good work to do. He's entrusted you with a child to raise—a child in your own image—who provides you with endless opportunities to show love and kindness. Look for those opportunities today. Walk into them with your eyes open, praising God for your purpose and His love.

PRAY:

Father, You don't make mistakes. You made me as a wonderful creation. Help me be part of Your plan for renewal in this world. Show me the good works You've prepared for me as a dad today. Give me the strength to do them well. Amen.

EQUIP YOURSELF FOR EVERY GOOD WORK

Read 2 Timothy 3

KEY VERSES:

All Scripture is God-breathed and is useful for teaching, rebuking, correcting and training in righteousness, so that the servant of God may be thoroughly equipped for every good work.

2 Timothy 3:16–17 NIV

UNDERSTAND:

According to today's passage, what will society look like in the last days?

....

....

....

What kind of treatment can righteous followers of God expect to get in these days?

....

....

....

How can you continue to learn and grow despite the persecutions you might face?

....

....

....

....

APPLY:

Great news! If you've finished reading this book, you're automatically a great dad and perfect Jesus follower!

Wait. No. Sadly, that's not true.

It would be great if reading a devotional once was all you needed, but that isn't how growing in your relationship with God works. That's like telling your children you love them when they are babies and never saying it again. We need constant reminders and interactions to show our love. And we need constant connection to God and His Word to be equipped for being dads in these dark days.

To stay immersed in God's Word, keep studying, keep memorizing scriptures. Start with these verses, and then find more on your own: Proverbs 14:26, Proverbs 23:24, Philippians 4:6, Titus 2:7–8, 3 John 1:4. Dig into them. Write them down. Live them out. Do it for your kids, for yourself, and for God's glory!

PRAY:

Lord, help me turn toward You and never stop growing in my faith. Help me continue studying Your Word so I can be equipped for every challenge and every good work. Amen.

ABOUT THE AUTHOR

Josh Mosey is the author of *3-Minute Prayers for Boys*, *Dare to be a Brave Boy*, *Man of Purpose*, and *Man of Honor*. He's the coauthor of *All of Creation: Understanding God's Planet and How We Can Help* (with Betsy Painter), *How to Fight Racism Young Reader's Edition* (with Jemar Tisby), *The Case for Christ: 365 Devotions for Kids* (with Lee Strobel), and *Men of Valor* (with Bob Evenhouse). Josh has contributed to other books for kids, teens, and grown-ups too. For a semi-complete listing of the books he's written, visit joshmosey.wordpress.com. Josh lives in the beautiful state of Michigan with his amazing family. He enjoys turning coffee into books and learning more about God.